JOHN BARR

Derelict Britain

PENGUIN BOOKS

Penguin Books Ltd, Harmondsworth, Middlesex, England
Penguin Books Inc., 7110 Ambassador Road, Baltimore, Md 21207, U.S.A.
Penguin Books Australia Ltd, Ringwood, Victoria, Australia

—

First published 1969

—

Copyright © John Barr, 1969

—

Made and printed in Great Britain
by Hazell Watson & Viney Ltd
Aylesbury, Bucks
Set in Linotype Baskerville

Contents

Acknowledgements   7

Part One: Squandered Acres

1 The Disgrace   11
2 The Badlands   38
3 The Obstacles   60

Part Two: Ravaged Valley

4 The Background   79
5 The Project   92
6 The Blueprint   109
7 The Prospects   130

Part Three: Redeemed Lands

8 The Successes   159
9 The Future   181
10 The Solutions   205
   A Note on Main Sources   227
   Index   232

List of Plates

1. 'Moonscape'. Part of a brick-works near Bedford (by courtesy of Bedfordshire County Council)
2. Careless Lane land-reclamation site, Ince-in-Makerfield (by courtesy of Lancashire County Council Planning Department)
3a. Littleburn planted pit heap (by courtesy of Durham County Council)
3b. Growth of trees on Littleburn waste heap (by courtesy of Durham County Council)
4a. Cossall tip as it appeared to passengers on the London-Sheffield railway line when the colliery closed in 1967 (by courtesy of Nottinghamshire County Council Planning Department)
4b. The same tip in July 1968 after re-grading work by the Nottinghamshire County Council Planning Department (by courtesy of Nottinghamshire County Council Planning Department)
5a. Cranford St John prior to restoration (by courtesy of Northamptonshire County Council)
5b. Cranford St John restored by Northamptonshire County Council 1954 (by courtesy of Northamptonshire County Council)
6. Mud, stones and rubble in an old quarry in the Lower Swansea Valley area (by courtesy of the *South Wales Evening Post*)
7. Looking across the river in the Lower Swansea Valley, with a view of industrial ruins and, in the background, the White Rock tip and part of Kilvey Hill (by courtesy of the *South Wales Evening Post*)
8a and 8b. A gravel pit at Sevenoaks, where trees have been planted to screen operations (by courtesy of the Civic Trust)
9. The spoil heap at Brodsworth Colliery (by courtesy of the Civic Trust and *Coal* magazine)
10. China-clay pit, Cornwall (Photo: T. P. Roskrow. By courtesy of the Civic Trust)
11. Gilfach Goch (by courtesy of the Welsh Office)

Part One: Squandered Acres

Acknowledgements

THIS book is a national study of industrial wastelands and
how to redeem them. But it has been inspired by the Lower
Swansea Valley Project, a discussion of which forms the central section of the book. I should therefore first like to thank
Robin Huws Jones, who originated the imaginative Swansea
project and who urged that this book should be written. All
those members of the staff of University College, Swansea, who
were involved in the project have been most helpful and two
of them – Gordon Goodman and Margaret Stacey – particularly exerted and perhaps exhausted themselves to assist me.
Steve Manchee, the project's conservator, made sure that I got
my feet dirty in the Lower Swansea Valley. Most of all, I am
grateful to Kenneth Hilton, who directed the project, for his
many lucid ideas about not only the valley but also the
national problem of derelict land. Several of the officers and
elected representatives of Swansea Corporation were also helpful, and I appreciate the assistance of the Nuffield Foundation, which generously supported the Swansea project.

Elsewhere, I have met some obstructive responses – but they
have been far fewer than I had anticipated. Various government departments have been helpful and, in particular, John
Oxenham, formerly at the Ministry of Housing and Local Government, went out of his way to satisfy my questions. The
Welsh Office and its derelict land unit were also co-operative.
At the local level, I have met consideration almost everywhere.
Specially valuable has been the assistance given me by the
county planning officers and their staffs in Bedfordshire, Cornwall, Durham, Lancashire, Northamptonshire, Nottinghamshire and the West Riding.

Among the industries which, for all my critical attitudes,
appreciated that I was not on a witch-hunt are the Central
Electricity Generating Board (in particular the staff of its

Acknowledgements

Peterborough reclamation scheme) and the Opencast Executive of the National Coal Board (notably its director-general, F. C. Baker). The Civic Trust and the Nature Conservancy have also been generous with help.

I should perhaps stress here that none of the persons or organizations whose assistance I acknowledge should be implicated in the views I am putting forward in this book.

Finally, I thank Timothy Raison for suggesting my name to Penguin Books, and most of all I thank my wife Pat both for encouraging me and for redeeming some of my derelict prose.

JOHN BARR

Chawston, Bedfordshire
February 1969

Chapter 1: The Disgrace

> Let us suppose that such a monstrous mountain had
> been built above Hampstead or Eton, where the
> children of the men of power and wealth are at
> school...
> — GWYNFOR EVANS, M.P. for Carmarthen

AT 9.15 in the morning of Friday 21 October 1966 an
avalanche of obscene coal sludge buried twenty-eight
adults and 116 children in the Welsh valley village of
Aberfan. After the immediate grief came the first questions. Writing of 'the disgust that such gargantuan waste
should have been piled at people's backyards', Dennis
Potter asked: 'Why should it be? Why is it thought necessary to be so loathsomely uncivilized?'

Those questions have not been answered – not by the
frightened men of the National Coal Board scuttling
about their other potential Aberfans, not by the Aberfan
Tribunal that condemned the creators of spoil tips, not
by the force of public opinion. 'And when the anger of
this tragedy has left the front pages,' wrote Potter, 'there is
more and still more and yet more to be angry about for a
place and a people like this.' But the anger is diluted now.
As a result of the disaster there has been a greater general
concern for safety by the guilty, a hurriedly organized
land-reclamation unit at the Welsh Office, and a self-
congratulatory Coal Board project to slice off the tops of
six tips and transform the graveyard of Aberfan into 'a
green parkland'. And finally, in July 1968, after twenty-
one months of pressure and pleading by the people of
Aberfan, the government grudgingly agreed to remove

the remaining tips, provided that the villagers contribute £250,000 towards the £1 million costs from the donations which flowed into Aberfan after the catastrophe.

Meanwhile, in a hundred other Welsh valleys and in hundreds of grey-black communities of the North and the Midlands, people continue to live amongst the spoil heaps of a dying industry. Some of the heaps are corpses, 'buried' atop not below the earth, their headstones the rusting winding gear and junk buildings of abandoned collieries. THERE'S A SECURE FUTURE IN MINING TODAY says a large and peeling hoarding outside one such scene, the empty Cleworth Colliery in south Lancashire. Other heaps are living (if that is the word), growing daily higher and fatter and more repulsive, the shale often smouldering, a gift of filthy smells for the people unfortunate enough to live beside them. Imagine a foul mountain growing by a million tons a year, ringed by evil, spreading slurry ponds – at Gedling Colliery in Nottinghamshire is one such scene. Dead or still growing, the heaps are monuments to man's degrading presence.

And it is not only the dirt dumps of man's lust for coal. Clay for pottery, clay for bricks, limestone and sand, sandstone and slate and chalk and gravel for building houses and building roads – all the extractive industries, essential for national prosperity, yet which gouge and tear the earth to bring out well over 400 million tons of usable minerals every year, the waste too often hurled about with no more conscience or discrimination than a toddler shows towards his just-smashed toys. If not cones as high as 300 feet or hogsback ridges half a mile long, then conical marlholes 300 feet deep or miles of raw scars on hillsides or lifeless man-made hillocks 100 feet down on the floors of clay pits or vast murky flashes where the ground has collapsed from man's gutting. Fifty-seven varieties, or more. Man's ingenuity turned to ways of ripping his landscape apart.

This dereliction kills vast acres of a small nation; at its ugliest it kills the spirit of the people who live amidst it, but it seldom kills in the way of Aberfan – at least not in the hundreds at one moment's blow, only a yearly trickle of too adventurous children who shouldn't have been playing round some abandoned mine shaft or steep-sided quarry.

Killing apart, the real point is that the industrial dereliction of Britain just shouldn't be there, shouldn't be tolerated. The holes should have been filled, the heaps dismantled, the scars healed – long ago. Sometimes they have been; too often they haven't been. So we have inherited a legacy of dereliction to add to the dereliction we are devising at this moment and the still greater dereliction we shall invent in the future. It is wrong that we should face all three problems. We should need to concern ourselves only with preventing the future despoliation; the past mess should be gone, the squandered acres recovered; the present mess should be under strict and programmed control, the disturbed land redeemed as swiftly as the minerals beneath it are exhausted. But, with a few happy exceptions, it isn't happening that way. Dereliction – so closely associated with the nineteenth-century industrial revolution – is actually increasing during our century of technological revolution.

This is happening despite this century's change of heart among many industrialists, of which the chairman of the Coal Board, Lord Robens, spoke – during the pre-Aberfan era when these words were more credible: 'In the early nineteenth century an industrialist saw only one responsibility: to get a sufficient return upon his capital. Now most industrialists would admit a responsibility to the community as a whole.' This is true of many modern industries, the socially awakened ones, but it is not true often enough. Despite new attitudes among many, dereliction is increasing because of the same old attitudes among many others. Jack Lowe, the county planner for Nottinghamshire, has summed up the root causes of to-day's as well as yesterday's dereliction: 'Desire for profit, often a quick one, in supplying the needs of a highly industrialized nation, coupled with a general apathy to-wards quality of environment.'

Official Dereliction

Muck = money – yesterday's unquestioned equation – has created some unpleasant arithmetic for us today: totting up the acres of Britain that are blighted or steri-lized by the mess of past industrial activities. Each year since 1964 the government has done this for England and Wales, based on estimates of dereliction supplied by local authorities. But the government's definition of derelict land * is so narrow and excludes so much that an average observer would consider derelict, that the official figures tell at most no more than half a bad story. Hugo Young in the *Sunday Times* has rightly attacked this government arithmetic: 'The official figures are compiled not to dis-cover how much dereliction there is, but to demonstrate how little the government need care about.'

Even so, the official figures are alarming enough. At the beginning of 1968 there were about 112,000 acres of officially derelict land in England and Wales – larger than the whole of Rutland or the combined municipal areas of Manchester, Cardiff and Birmingham. In Scotland there

*See Chapter 2.

were another estimated 15,000 acres of dereliction – an area larger than the cities of Dundee or Aberdeen.

This long-standing dereliction (for that is all that the government figures measure) is being added to substantially each year; enlightened reclamation * schemes are outstripped by unenlightened new despoliation. The Civic Trust has estimated the *net* addition to derelict land at 3,500 acres annually. Professor Gerald Wibberley has estimated the annual *gross* rate of land loss to mineral workings at about 12,000 acres, of which nearly half is first-class farmland. The government's own statistics of industrial dereliction have shown, since 1964, yearly increases in England and Wales of as little as 1,340 and as much as 8,000 acres. And a really realistic total of past and present dereliction – widening the government's definition, yet restricting it to man-made dereliction – would probably show that in Britain today there are something like 250,000 squandered acres – about the area of the county of Huntingdonshire. And derelict land is nearly always bang in the middle of intensively populated areas, its impact out of all proportion to its actual acreage.

Put in terms of the proportion of the land area of Britain, even this total can console those who seek consolation: only about one half of one per cent of the nation's land is derelict as a result of man's works. Yet in this tight little island, our population growing by more than 1,000 a day, to waste even this much land is both

---

* The Civic Trust has drawn attention to the distinction, in official documents, sometimes drawn between the 'reclamation' of derelict land for some necessary development; its 'restoration' to its original farming use; and its visual 'rehabilitation' by landscaping and planting. Except when necessary to avoid ambiguity, I shall use these terms – and 'renewal' and 'redemption' and other approximate synonyms – interchangeably.

stupid and scandalous. The pressures on our land today are too great for any profligacy. The government estimated in early 1966 that by the year 2000 there would be 19 million more people in England and Wales. Wibberley, warning of land scarcity in Britain, has predicted that the man/land ratio in the year 2000 will be well over 1,000 persons per square mile, compared to 790 in 1961. By 2000 six million acres (or 16 per cent) of England and Wales will be urbanized, compared to four million acres (or 11 per cent) in 1960. In England and Wales there is now only 0·8 acre per head of population of land of all sorts. For production of food, there is less than 0·5 acre a head.* Wibberley's verdict: 'We are too small a country to turn our back on the wastes we make.' The late Sir

* Robin Best and J. T. Coppock have estimated that the net loss of farmland in England and Wales to all other uses, including mineral workings, was about seven per cent during the first half of this century. Wibberley has predicted that by the year 2000 the area of agricultural crops and grass in England and Wales is likely to be less by about fifteen to twenty per cent of its acreage in 1900. Nearly always the best grade of agricultural land is used for mineral extraction. This means that the loss to agriculture is all the more serious. More encouraging statistics, issued by the Ministry of Agriculture in 1968, show that the loss of farming land to industry and urban development has now been balanced by regaining land from the Services and by improving for crops and grass land previously classified as rough grazing. How long this balance can be maintained is questionable. Of course agricultural production has been rising despite shrinking acreage. The Association of British Manufacturers of Agricultural Chemicals, which reckons that 1·5 million acres of farmland in the U.K. have been lost to urban and industrial development since the war, points out that the net volume of agricultural output is today nearly double what it was before the war and the extra production is worth some £400 million a year. The contribution to helping our balance of payments is obvious. But if farmlands continue to shrink it is also questionable how long intensive farming and agricultural chemicals can maintain the growth.

Dudley Stamp's conclusion: 'There should be no such thing as waste land.'

New Demands on Land

The competing demands on land in Britain today – and even more tomorrow – make these conclusions imperative. Our growing population is, more and more, a car-owning, leisure-seeking, house-buying population, with sophisticated possessions and pursuits that make even greater claims on land than the simple increase in bodies would suggest.

There are now about 16 million motor vehicles on our roads; by 1980 there may be 27 million, by the year 2000 some 40 million more. There are more than 200,000 miles of roads already; ever greater slices of the countryside will have to be taken to accommodate ever more vehicles.

What Michael Dower has called 'the Fourth Wave' * – the leisure boom – is already upon us; without careful land use, that wave may swamp us. By the year 2000 Britons, working on average 30–35-hour weeks, may take some 60 million holidays – usually in their private cars. Already our coastline is overcrowded at holidays and weekends, its beauties despoiled or threatened by too many people. Already some of our national parks and areas of outstanding beauty – especially the Lake and the Peak districts – have reached the limits of their capacities to absorb holidaymakers in cars.

Many of the leisure pursuits which are growing most rapidly in popularity are those which require space, lots of space. Water sports, skiing, camping, caravanning, golf.

* Dower's earlier three waves: the sudden growth of dark industrial towns, the thrusting movement along far-flung railways, and the sprawl of car-based suburbs.

There are already more than a million golfers and 2,000 courses; the Central Council of Physical Recreation says the average 18-hole course covers nearly 100 acres. The National Playing Fields Association estimates that golfers are increasing at a rate of nine per cent a year: 'If this is taken literally, it will mean that we shall be requiring four acres per 1,000 of population for golf courses alone.'

We are now building more than 400,000 new dwellings a year. The recurring annual needs for new homes (apart from the millions of homes to replace slums and dwellings not worth improving, and to overcome shortages) have been officially estimated at 30,000 units a year to replace the loss caused by road-widenings and other redevelopment and 150,000 a year just to keep up with new households being formed in the rising, earlier-marrying generation. When slums and near-slums are replaced by decent homes, they almost inevitably require more land. There has been an understandable reaction against high-rise blocks of flats designed to pack a lot of people on a small chunk of land. And though low-rise, high-density housing developments capable of accommodating as many as 140 people an acre are now fashionable, the ambition of many – perhaps most – people remains a semi with a garage and a garden of their own. Add to this very human desire, our rising expectations: probably a house of at least 1,000 square feet floor space, where a decade ago something smaller would have done.

Like modern housing, modern industry requires ever greater bites of our limited land. A new electricity generating station requires 500 acres, an oil refinery 1,000 acres or more, a North Sea gas terminal about 200 acres. New airports to accommodate the jumbo jets and supersonics of the 1970s will need to be created and will devour vast areas. If an inland site – Wing, Nuthampstead or Thurleigh – is chosen as London's third airport, concrete runways, houses, roads, airport buildings will affect 10,000 acres of now rural land. Add to all this new schools and universities to meet both population growth and the rising demands for more education, car parks, hospitals, shops and offices – and the demands on Britain's 88,000 square miles become frightening. To tolerate any needlessly derelict land is a disgrace. By renewing the acres spoiled by man we can at least contribute to solving our crisis of space. Not to do this is to waste our national resources.

Vital Minerals

This plea does not contradict the importance of minerals to the nation's prosperity. It is inappropriate to adopt a narrowly 'anti' view, complete with the conditioned reflex that triggers a quick No at the very word 'mineral'. The 'anywhere ... except here' approach is unhelpful. Minerals must be worked. They must be worked where they exist – though this seemingly irrefutable truism can sometimes be modified. While Sir Dudley Stamp believed that 'undoubtedly the prior claimant to allocation of land is industry' (an arguable conclusion if extended to all circumstances) he also pointed out that some minerals – chalk, limestone, brick clay, sand and gravel – are in such abundant supply that 'industries using these raw materials can be the subject of deliberately planned location'. Also, as Jack Lowe has noted, 'There are areas within each mineral field where restoration or after-use is more certain than elsewhere, and future operations should be systematically channelled to such sites.'

Such sensible *planning* of mineral extraction happens

too seldom, partly because for every local authority which stands up to industry and, within the limits of common sense and legal powers, directs and controls mineral workings, there are ten local authorities who are cowed by industry and exercise little or no direction and control. Industry puts up a front, lots of smooth public relations about 'preserving the countryside', and it leads too many planning officers by the nose. This is unsurprising. For one thing, many local councils cannot see beyond the rateable value which industry brings: 'amenity' is not in their vocabularies. Also, they appreciate that land-reclamation is generally considered a dull issue and is not, like housing or education, a vote-getter. And in any case many local authorities simply lack the initiative and the officers of a calibre to resist highly professional vested interests. One Ministry of Housing officer admits: 'The vested interests pull so much weight ... if a local authority protests, they get the best Q.C.s and usually that's that.'

This namby-pamby approach by so many local authorities would matter much less if central government were prepared to be firm (but fair) with industry and if it were truly committed to the redemption of land disfigured by industry. In fact, successive governments have exhibited a deplorable lack of will on this issue; their lack of commitment has found its scapegoat in that nebulous thing called 'public opinion'. In his foreword to the government's first earnest look at the problem of dereliction – the booklet *New Life for Dead Lands*, published in 1963 – Sir Keith Joseph, the Minister of Housing and Local Government at the time, wrote: 'So far the force of public opinion has been insufficient to stimulate a widespread attack on derelict land whether by public or private agencies.'

Today government officials, when pressed on their failure really to tackle dereliction, nod resignedly, smile evasively and make much the same excuses. While it is true that there is a growing national *recognition* of dereliction, there is still no national *will* to remove it. But on many issues – and derelict land is one of them – it is surely central government's job to lead actively not respond passively to 'public opinion'. Though a clear majority of the people condemned to live in Derelict Britain are traditionally Labour supporters, Harold Wilson's government has shown no more determination than the Tories to shape public opinion on this issue and sweep away the mess left after private enterprise had wrung its profits from the earth.

Instead, the government disguises its passivity with tiresome litanies about 'the national interest'. Minerals are a measurable national wealth; a decent environment is not. It is all too familiar a proposition. In the early 1970s our windows and our ear-drums are to be shattered by the Concorde 'in the national interest'. London is to have a third airport, no matter the human discomfort involved, 'in the national interest'. The idea that technological progress and prosperity must inevitably bring with them despoliation of the environment is now a much-challenged but not yet dislodged assertion.

Yet the challenges accumulate. Dr E. J. Mishan, in his brilliant assault on the icons of conventional economic theories, *The Costs of Economic Growth*, wrote:

Our environment is sinking fast into a welter of disamenities, yet the most vocal part of the community cannot raise their eyes from the trade figures to remark the painful event. Notwithstanding the fact that bringing the Jerusalem of economic growth to England's green and pleasant land has so far conspicuously reduced both the greenness and the pleasantness, economic growth remains the most respectable catchword in the current political vocabulary.

The Civic Trust's pamphlet *Eyesores* notes that our 'shrinking countryside is scarred and disfigured by man-made ugliness of every kind' and asks, 'Must progress and ugliness go hand in hand? Have we got to accept that drabness and disorder are the price we must pay for prosperity?' The report, in 1966, of the environment committee of the North West Economic Planning Council argued that 'Dirt has brought to the people of this region many other things in its wake besides "brass" – including sickness, drabness and all sorts of human problems.' The report called the industrial muck of the North West 'retribution imposed on the third and fourth generations ... although today this squalor is no longer a price we have to pay for progress and prosperity'. No doubt the government could shrug off such challenges by considering Mishan a very 'quirky' economist, the Civic Trust a collection of 'soft-boiled preservationists', the North West Planning Council as just another 'vested interest' with its eyes on Exchequer handouts.

Government Aid

In fact, spasmodically since the war the government *has* operated a grants scheme * to encourage local authorities to reclaim or at least to landscape derelict land. At times the grants have been tied to providing jobs in areas of high unemployment; areas with much dereliction but only average unemployment have not qualified. Most of the time grants have been restricted to development districts or development areas; not until April 1967 were all parts of the country brought under a grants scheme – and

* Details in Chapter 3.

outside development areas the grant offered is only fifty per cent of the acquisition and reclamation costs, an insufficient incentive for the small and poor local authorities which so often are the very ones with the greatest problems of dereliction. The grants have followed the swings of the national economy, indeed almost anticipated the low swings; so low on the priority list is the reclamation of derelict land that it is one of the first victims of the Exchequer's razor. No sooner was the more liberal grants scheme of April 1967 introduced than the Ministry of Housing rushed out a circular announcing that because of the economic squeeze applications for reclamation schemes designed to create open space would not be entertained; future uses for reclaimed land had to be industry or housing.

In April 1968 this ban on 'green schemes' was quietly lifted, though this time the ministry did not send out a circular, for fear that too many authorities would take advantage of the liberalization. Many local authorities probably don't know today that they can again submit reclamation projects to create playing fields or parkland. It is true that at intervals since the war the government has invited, even urged, local authorities to resurrect their dead lands, but there is still no statutory obligation upon them to do so. Until there is a positive obligation, the government's professed determination to rid the nation of its ugliest lands carries little conviction and when the present Minister of Housing and Local Government, Anthony Greenwood, speaks of 'strong evidence to suggest that the long-awaited upsurge in reclamation schemes will be forthcoming', no one really believes him.

Land reclamation clearly arouses little enthusiasm in Whitehall. 'At the national level the policy seems to be to accept that there is a problem,' says Richard Atkinson,

County Durham's planning officer, 'but not to give it any kind of priority or to want to solve it within a stated and limited time.' It is perhaps symbolic that the tiny team of Ministry of Housing people who are concerned with derelict land are not even housed in Whitehall, but near St James's Park in the dusty tomb-like Queen Anne's Mansions, itself semi-derelict. This capable but low-powered team is patently not equipped, nor charged, to produce a national blueprint for reclamation, only to advise on technical problems of reclamation * and to add up the official yearly statistics of dereliction. Nor does it have the powers to chivvy local authorities into action. And certainly the mass of apathetic authorities need chivvying. As one county planner puts it: 'There are about six counties who are carrying the torch, and there are probably not more than about thirty or forty people in the whole country who are playing an effective and active part in countering dereliction.' Here it is significant that the most thorough study of an area of dereliction, resulting in the most detailed blueprint for action in the nation – the Lower Swansea Valley Project – has been done not by a 'down-to-earth' local authority nor by 'purposeful' central government but by the supposed 'ivory-tower academics' at the University College of Swansea.

Splendid Spoil Heaps

A corollary of this widespread inertia at both national and local levels is the notion that people get used to living amidst dereliction, that they come not to see it, that they

---

* The Ministry of Agriculture maintains a land-restoration committee which also gives valuable advice on farming restored derelict land.

come even to love it all: the spoil heaps that ring them, the holes on their doorsteps, the subsided land about them which sometimes results in their houses being held together with stout steel bands. This is part of the same middle-class philosophy which once concluded that there was no need to give the working classes baths as they'd only use them for storing coal. This dictum did not stand the test of time. And just as the working classes of yesterday quickly learned to reject the wooden tub by the kitchen fire and regard the bathroom as a rightful necessity, so today's workers are rejecting the grimy, inconvenient surroundings of their parents and demanding as a right cleaner towns, cleaner air, cleaner land. It is some academic opinion-makers, usually living far from the nearest spoil heap, who defend dereliction on aesthetic grounds. To them and, one suspects, to them alone, reclamation is seen as an enemy of the wondrous heaps and holes and tears-in-the-hillsides which shout proudly MAN WAS HERE! Certainly some of man's dereliction does have a fantastical, madly impressive quality, so ruinous that it is monumental; undoubtedly a few bits here and there should be retained as open-air museums of industrial archaeology. (And some quarries should certainly be left untouched for the joy of geologists and very many wet gravel pits should be left to the water fowl and the bird-watchers.) Certainly every industrial county should not be refashioned to imitate every agricultural one.

But in an attack on the Civic Trust's 1964 publication, *Derelict Land*, the architectural correspondent Ian Nairn argued against filling 'the colossal and dramatic clay excavations' near Peterborough, praised the china-clay works round Bugle in Cornwall, romanticized the gigantic shale 'bings' between Edinburgh and Glasgow, got

heated about plans to landscape a massive pit heap in
Lancashire: 'a splendid piece of landscape here and now'.
This is preciousness masquerading as muscularity.
Richard Atkinson, speaking before Nairn's defence of
soul-stirring messes, anticipated the answer:

One hears about the sculptural form of a pit heap or the
way it 'punctuates' the landscape or about the charm of a disused industrial structure. Of course I see the point. But I must
say that I am myself much more conscious of the beastliness
and brutality of some of our industrial scenes. There is a great
deal which is not romantic in the slightest degree and which
blights and degrades the environment in which so many live
their lives.

Confrontation and Connivance

More disturbing than this splendid-spoil-heap philosophy, to which few subscribe, is the growing confrontation on the issue of industry's assaults on the landscape
between industrialists on the one hand, planning authorities and amenity groups on the other. The considerable
body of enlightened industrialists have no part in this
confrontation – quite the contrary. But in the minerals
extraction industry – generally a rough-and-tumble, old-
fashioned industry with more than its share of obsolete
attitudes – the spokesmen for the industry are too often
hostile and contemptuous of planning officers and civic
groups, whom they consider 'amateurs'. John Taylor,
director of Associated Portland Cement Manufacturers,
is the leading exponent of such views. At the 1967
national conference of the Council for the Preservation of
Rural England, Taylor told a startled audience that local
planning authorities had only the slightest acquaintance

with the complex problems of mineral workings,* that their uninformed interference was intolerable, and that their only true function was 'to provide a free flow of minerals which undertakers can work effectively'.

In September 1967, a sub-group of the Countryside in 1970 Committee (set up by the Duke of Edinburgh in 1963) produced an astonishing document on industry's 'so-called inroads into the countryside'. The sub-group – which was composed of four industrialists – complacently concluded that the damage 'is less extensive than the sub-group anticipated, and much less than might be believed from the publicity given to many industrial development'. There were hints of a kind of national conspiracy against minerals undertakers. The report found planning controls on industry irksome and attacked 'well-organized pressure groups and well-meaning but ill-informed individuals'. It admitted that the planning procedure 'encourages formal (and expensive) confrontation rather than amicable discussion', but it rejected any idea of a code of practice for industry and conservationists to follow when industrial developments affecting the countryside are contemplated. It came to the dispiriting conclusion that 'the aims of industry and conservationist bodies are too dissimilar ... it would be impossible to devise anything at all meaningful'.

This whitewash document was all the more depressing for carrying the imprint and prestige of the Countryside in 1970, which in recent years has done much admirable work and fostered amicable exchanges of ideas among

---

*This is sometimes true, though decreasingly so. Today most planning authorities of any size and strength have on their staffs minerals officers familiar with the economics and realities of minerals extraction; indeed, many of them are too knowledgeable for the liking of minerals operators.

planners, industry and preservationists. It may be, as one defender of the sub-group report claims, 'an achievement that industry even goes to the trouble of making such a report'. But if – in the face of statistics clearly indicating that industrial dereliction is increasing by thousands of acres a year – a reputable group of industrialists insists on contending that twentieth-century industry is scarcely hurting the landscape, such a report is worse than none at all.

Such a report broadcasts a misconception that even some professional planners surprisingly accept and themselves promote. D. W. Riley, a former Staffordshire county planning officer, has written: 'The creation of new areas of dereliction is now largely prevented by imposing restoration conditions on permissions for new mineral workings.' Yet there are many instances, such as the ever-increasing holes in the Oxford Clay brickfields, the growing spoil mountains outside practically every working colliery (each year the NCB dumps an estimated 60 million tons of spoil on to the land), the unsightly Niagara of deep-mine filth hurled over the cliffs each year on to the beaches of Durham – all instances of new areas of dereliction where the planning authorities are helpless and cannot impose restoration conditions, either because filling materials at reasonable prices are not available or because the spoilers escape all planning controls under the General Development Order which, amazingly, even now permits continued and unrestrained tipping on any site which was so used in July 1948.

Better-informed planners do not 'buy' complacent conclusions; they recognize and regret this growing confrontation between planners and the reactionary elements in industry. Richard Atkinson sums up the situation this way:

Planning officers up and down the country know that there are still vast numbers of instances in which industry take the view that planners and control are unnecessary interferences with their activities and that anything which adds a halfpenny to their bills must be resisted at all costs. There is no doubt that, in many ways, *the position is getting worse rather than better*.

While some (certainly not all) industrialists choose to whitewash their assaults on the landscape, the government stands passively by, indeed appears to connive – no doubt 'in the national interest'. Any government officials who, in speeches or writings, wish to attack the irresponsible sectors of industry for needlessly despoiling the land find their tongues muzzled, their texts emasculated. For a frank and serious evaluation of the problem of dereliction to emerge with government blessing involves a gross of blue pencils and months or years of shuttling through the in- and out-trays of administrative-class civil servants. At all costs, industry must not be too sharply criticized. The nation's welfare depends on profit: the hole-makers and heap-makers are sacrosanct.

In some instances the government's connivance with industry reaches the absurd point where not only are legitimate profits fostered, but illegitimate ones as well. In the Oxford Clay brickfields, the Ministry of Housing's own ambiguously worded planning conditions * permit the brick-makers not only rightly to realize a profit on what they remove from the earth but a profit on the very holes themselves. Local authorities which dump town-refuse in the pits pay for the privilege; the Central Electricity Generating Board, which is restoring some of the pits by filling them with power-station ash, pays for its admirable redemption – and when the restoration is

*See Chapter 9.

done, the brick companies will make a considerable additional profit by selling the regained acres for development. Local ratepayers and all the nation's electricity consumers are in effect subsidizing the brick industry. The government has done nothing to halt this scandal, nor to put an end to profiteering by the owners of holes near urban areas who refuse to entertain any reclamation schemes simply because a derelict dry pit is more valuable than just about anything which might replace it. As Aylmer Coates, Lancashire's chief planner, puts it: 'The most expensive land near Salford is a hole in the ground ... owners charge 2s. 6d. a ton to tip. As a tipping-site the land is worth £1,250 an acre ... as good farmland maybe £150.'

Prohibitive Costs?

Immediate and measurable financial gain: this is also the philosophy which too often governs industry's and central and local government's thinking about land reclamation. Not 'Could the land serve a useful purpose?' or simply 'Would it look better?' but 'Will it pay us to reclaim it?' and, most of all, 'How much will it cost us to do it?' Cost-benefit analysis is still a primitive art in Britain and – with the prominent exception of the Lower Swansea Valley report and a handful of other studies of local dereliction – the less tangible and *long-term social benefits* of land reclamation simply haven't been investigated.

The Civic Trust has pointed out: 'Beauty has an economic value, ugliness has an economic cost.' A study group at the 1965 conference of the Countryside in 1970 concluded: 'The control of dereliction should be recognized as being of equal social consequence as other forms of environmental control: clean streets, clean air and clean rivers.' Perhaps both these bodies were too far out-pacing 'public opinion' and government thinking. Per-haps they were too impatient. Perhaps we must wait a few decades more before their message takes root in the corridors of power.

John Oxenham, formerly the official adviser on land reclamation to the Ministry of Housing and Local Gov-ernment, has said in his authoritative book *Reclaiming Derelict Land*: 'Cost has always been held up as the deterrent to every social improvement.' He cited Acts of Parliament requiring clean water, sewerage, clean air – all of them delayed not for decades but for centuries beyond the recognition of the evils they finally attacked. And to-day – though industrial dereliction may be recognized as an evil – 'It will cost too much ... we just can't afford it' is the frequent response at all levels of government to suggestions that a determined, military type of operation be started to restore or landscape at least the hard core of dereliction left from the industrial revolution – the 80,000 or so acres in Britain which the government itself con-siders to 'justify treatment'. Britain's current economic difficulties are of course frequently cited, because they are a strong argument for doing nothing. Yet it is all too apparent that the economic squeeze is a convenient pre-text for a government which really doesn't want to act, and a pretext positively welcomed by those many apathetic local authorities who simply don't want to know about the problem of dereliction.

Estimates of how much a ten-year reclamation pro-gramme of the worst of the existing dereliction would cost range from £20 million to £60 million: about £35 million is now a widely accepted figure, based on the costs in-curred by a few enlightened authorities, such as Lanca-shire, which have gone ahead with land renewal despite the lack of incentives. This works out at little more than a shilling per head of population per year. Can we not afford this much to rehabilitate our environment? Perhaps one trouble is that industrial dereliction is a gradual, insidious degradation; when a sudden, brutal attack on this beautiful island occurs – such as the Torrey Canyon oil-tanker disaster in 1967 – millions are somehow produced overnight to save the nation from despoliation. Can we not afford £35 million over ten years? This nation of gardeners spends about that amount *each year* on seeds, plants, shrubs, ornamental trees – on things to enhance the *private* environment. This nation of pet-keepers spends nearly that much *each year* on pet accessories – feeding bowls, dog beds, catnip mice, budgie toys – designed to improve the environment of our 13 million cats, dogs and caged birds.

The question too seldom asked is, 'What is it costing us *not* to renew our dead lands?' That is the proper question. The answers are so apparent that it makes our inaction all the more disgraceful.

Effects of Dereliction

First of all, industrial wastelands are a visual affront. They offend the eye, they offend what is one of the world's most civilized landscapes. More than thirty years ago Thomas Sharp wrote: 'A landscape is an index to a civilization.' To tolerate dereliction spattering that landscape, to expect people to live amidst dereliction, is not civilized.

Derelict land, and the industrial junk left behind when industry has made its profit and fled, is dangerous to life. Robert Howarth, M.P. for Bolton East, raised this point during an adjournment debate (on derelict sites) in the Commons in April 1967. He cited examples of children

killed in abandoned cotton mills, drowned in disused
canals or while playing on frozen flashes, the treacherous
ponds that collect on ground subsided from mining. In
Bolton in April 1968 three girls and a fireman coming to
their rescue were killed by gas accumulated in a disused
colliery. It was not the Coal Board's fault, but it pointed
up the constant danger to life of the tens of thousands of
sealed mine entrances in the country. In 1966, according
to the Royal Society for the Prevention of Accidents, there
were 227 accidental deaths in Great Britain in mines and
quarries, including seventeen children under fifteen years
of age, eleven of whom drowned. Not all of those children
died necessarily in *derelict* mines and quarries, but it can
be assumed that a majority did.

Derelict land – and the assorted rubbish which its
ugliness and uselessness attracts – is dangerous to health.
The British Ecological Society has pointed out that reclamation is sometimes required not for commercial or
recreational reasons but simply on public health grounds,
to eliminate flies and vermin and to remove the nuisance
of dust. At the 1967 annual conference of the Association
of Public Health Inspectors, John Stephenson noted sor-
rowfully: 'The easiest and cheapest way to dispose of
refuse is to find a large hole in the ground, empty the
rubbish into it and beat a hasty retreat.' This method of
crude tipping was still used in 1967 by no fewer than 115
local authorities, and another 460 authorities got rid of
their rubbish by 'semi-controlled' tipping, often little
better. While thoroughly controlled tipping of town
refuse can make a valuable contribution to land reclamation, these primitive methods only further aggravate
already repulsive dereliction and create public health
problems. Dereliction is a magnet for more dereliction.

Derelict land, in an age of rising aspirations and growing demands for a better environment, contributes to depopulation, to the migration – particularly of the young – to areas less debased by industrial mess. And much of the nation's dereliction is in the development areas or 'grey' districts of northern England and Wales, the very places to which the government is attempting to entice people. A 1968 study of dereliction in the West Riding by the county planning department has established a correlation between outward migration from districts of high spoliation and inward migration to areas of low spoliation, especially among young females. John Casson, the county's deputy planning officer, believes TV advertising and films are setting new, materialistically higher physical standards and that young people in the drab old areas of the country increasingly seek those higher standards elsewhere. He also raises a point often lost sight of by planners in Whitehall: 'By leaving the dereliction here [and so contributing to outward migration] we are escalating the pressures on, say, Buckinghamshire.'

Derelict land, and the wider degraded environment of which it is so often a part and to which it contributes, is a deterrent to modern industry. Top executives – and even more, perhaps, their wives – are much more reluctant than trees or grass to put down their roots in shale heaps and arsenical soil. Casson, and L. A. King, West Riding's forestry officer, told the British Association for the Advancement of Science at its 1967 conference: 'The most powerful stimulus to the flow of capital under modern conditions is first-class environment ... without environment renewal the North may be condemned to increasing dependence on the older and declining staple industries.' In County Durham, Richard Atkinson has found: 'Industrialists are increasingly critical of the environment in which they choose to establish new projects, and potential industrial developments have been lost from parts [of Durham] simply because the quality of town or landscape was not good enough for them.'

Widespread dereliction can contribute to the decline of a whole region. In its evidence to the Hunt Committee on 'grey' areas, the Yorkshire and Humberside Economic Planning Council spoke of 'serious environmental handicaps in some parts of the region ... outworn urban and industrial fabric, and a lot of derelict land. All spell economic decline.' And so areas of high industrial spoliation come to an unhappy concatenation of events: dereliction contributes to the exodus of workers and of modern industries already established there, and dereliction also discourages other modern industries from coming. As the government itself put it in *New Life for Dead Lands*: 'Desolate, unkempt land may not be only a symptom of obsolescence, it may also be the cause of it.'

Derelict land sours its surroundings. A spoil tip threatens a much larger area than that on which it perches like some vile bird of prey. A series of heaps or holes in an area kill the interstices as well. Dereliction depreciates – in all senses – the value of land in its vicinity; it helps to create what we have come to call 'twilight' areas. A report in 1965 by a subcommittee of planning officers in the North East described the character of such areas: 'A sense of apathy towards the living environment ... houses not repainted, fences left to rot, kerbs broken, trees hacked about mercilessly, gardens unkempt and unused open spaces a mass of long grass, weeds and rubbish.' The East Midlands Economic Planning Council has referred to 'the abandoned factory and the marshalling yard which was associated with it, the waste land which may lie between it and the road or the railway, all the old outhouses and the heaps of rusting machinery which may have been abandoned ... it needs very little of this to cast a gloom upon an area'.

It is then costing us dearly *not* to clear away the legacy of past industry. It is going to cost us yet more dearly if we do not prevent present and future dereliction. The study by the North East planning officers cited the 'belching lime kilns and working quarries' in the region and warned: 'There is little point in clearing up dereliction and untidiness ... if working areas, equally large and prominent, are not also considered. Unless this problem is tackled, the present working areas will become the future dereliction.' And John Oxenham has warned: 'There may well be more dereliction within the next twenty or thirty years than has accumulated during the past century.'

Manifesto

These warnings will become realities unless we mount a national campaign to reclaim or landscape our squandered acres. We have the machines and the technical expertise to do the job. We must find the money. This campaign will require, among many things, a national land-reclamation agency with sufficient powers, a national land-reclamation fund with sufficient resources, and a Clean Land Act with sufficient teeth to require that the job be done.*

Until then, industrial dereliction will continue to be – alongside air-pollution, noise-making and water-pollution, all of which are at least under some controls – a major contributor to the degradation of our environment by ourselves. On purely economic grounds, land reclamation also makes sense. To tolerate hundreds of thousands of derelict acres is bad land use, bad conserva-

* Detailed proposals in Chapter 10.

tion of our most important natural resource: the land itself. Says Robert Boote, deputy director of the Nature Conservancy: 'Failing to conserve is itself a source of inefficiency.'

Our tolerance of industrial dereliction is one of the inefficiencies which has prevented Britain from fully entering the twentieth century. It will surely exclude us from full and efficient participation in the twenty-first century. Unless we do something about it. Now.

Chapter 2: The Badlands

Who can ever express the desolation of these forlorn scenes? The grey slag heaps, the acres of land littered with rusted fragments of machinery ... vile buildings, more vile in ruin ... the air about them still so foul that nothing more than a few nettles and tattered thistles will grow there. This is the worst that has happened to the land.

— JACQUETTA HAWKES *A Land*

IF the strictly legal definition of derelict land ruled our actions – 'land which has been relinquished or abandoned by its owner' – the possibilities of reclamation would scarcely arise. Owners seldom abandon even the most unpromising snippet of earth so long as its smouldering shale or straggly grasses could realize a penny's profit. 'It is truly amazing,' says one county planner, 'how piles of rubbish change into pots of gold the moment a planning officer casts his eye on them.' Fortunately the government's working definition of industrial dereliction is more liberal: 'Land so damaged by industrial or other development that it is incapable of beneficial use without treatment.'

To the man in the street (or, more appropriately, on some desolate stretch vandalized by industry) this definition may appear admirable, combining the virtues of succinctness and all-inclusiveness. As the Countryside in 1970 conference said:

To most of us 'derelict land' means virtually any land which is ugly or unattractive in appearance: spoil heaps, scrap or rubbish dumps, excavations, dilapidated buildings, subsided

38

or war-damaged land or any land which is neglected, unused or even under-used.

The official definition *could* include all such testimonies to man's ill works. But it doesn't. For purposes of entertaining grants for reclamation or improvements of derelict land, the government appends to its definition a cluster of exceptions which effectively removes at least half the nation's dereliction from any consideration.

The official definition does include *disused* spoil heaps, *worked out* mineral excavations, *abandoned* industrial premises, and land *already* damaged by subsidence. It even includes 'neglected or unsightly land, which meets the criterion of past and completed dereliction'. But the official definition does not include 'land in active use for any purpose'. This monumental exception means that land damaged by industry but which is subject to conditions attached to planning permissions or other statutory arrangements requiring restoration or landscaping escapes the definition. This means that land, such as that covered by spoil tips, which is still being used for tipping escapes the definition. This means that land damaged by development but which is subject to planning permission for further development or on which further development will take place under the existing permission 'in the foreseeable future' escapes the definition.

Just three of many possible examples illustrate how incomplete a picture of our dereliction is given by the government's statistics, based as they are on such an exception-ridden definition. In Bedfordshire, on 31 December 1967, only 635 acres of the county were officially derelict. In fact, the monstrous pits being worked, or already worked out, by the brick-makers covered 1,400 acres. The pits are not considered 'derelict' because planning conditions providing for after-treatment are attached to them;

but the planning authority cannot impose the conditions and, short of a radical regional or national reclamation rescue-operation, there is no hope that the pits will ever be reclaimed. In Nottinghamshire, on 31 December 1967, 2,014 acres of the county were officially derelict. In fact coal spoil heaps and stinking slurry ponds covered 2,500 acres. Under the General Development Order much of the spoliation is outside any control by the county planning authority. In Aberfan, on 21 October 1966, Tip Seven at Merthyr Vale Colliery was not officially derelict; it was a tip in active use. It was indeed 'land in active use for any purpose'.

The Blight

Yet even by the official statistics, on the last day of 1967 (the latest available figures) there were in England 92,643 derelict acres, of which 56,841 were deemed to justify 'treatment' – that is, either restoration or landscaping. In Wales there were 19,785 acres, of which 13,272 could be treated – and there were 2,355 derelict acres in national parks and areas of outstanding natural beauty. In October 1966 the Scottish Development Department estimated that there were 15,000 derelict acres in Scotland; it can be assumed that about 10,000 were capable of treatment.*

In England a year earlier there were 92,876 derelict acres; the year before that, 90,986. In Wales, at the end of 1966 there were 18,212 acres; the year before 16,000.

---

*The Ministry of Development for Northern Ireland says: 'A complete survey of derelict land in Northern Ireland has not been made, but the information we have suggests that the extent of the problem is not great. We do not, for example, have to deal with industrial spoil heaps on any scale and dereliction in the countryside is mainly local in character and confined to small areas.'

The growth of dereliction which these figures suggest is in part accounted for by increasingly sophisticated – or at least less casual – surveys by local authorities. Many areas of dereliction which existed in 1964 may not have appeared in the national totals until 1966 or even 1967. On the other hand, since the statistics measure only the legacy of past industrial activities and do not include the current despoliation, and since most mineral undertakings are steadily and sometimes spectacularly growing each year, the actual annual increase is without doubt much greater than the government's surveys imply. In any case, as one government official himself admits: 'The survey is not really designed to know how much dereliction there is – the government doesn't want to know about that – but only how much it will cost.'

What the statistics do more accurately, and even more depressingly, indicate is that reclamation or landscaping is moving at a dawdling pace. In England in 1964, 2,076 acres were dealt with; works during 1965 were proposed for another 3,540 acres. During 1965 only 2,061 acres were treated, and there were plans to deal with 4,595 acres in 1966. But in 1966 a still smaller acreage – only 1,641 – was treated, but there were proposals for 3,910 acres during 1967. In Wales in 1966 only 201 acres were treated, none at all in nine counties with derelict acreage; work on 1,116 acres was scheduled for 1967. In view of the government's ban on reclamation schemes solely for amenity, in force during most of 1967, the results that year were unsurprisingly poor; only 1,639 acres in England and 229 acres in Wales were reclaimed or landscaped.

Some of the more afflicted areas have pathetic records of reclamation. During 1967 the North Riding, with 1,109 acres officially considered to justify reclamation or landscaping, treated a total of 4 acres; Cheshire, with

1,299 such acres, treated 5; Cumberland (2,208 acres) treated 2; Lindsey, Lincolnshire (2,668) treated none; Northumberland (6,531) treated 49. In England, of 100 counties and county boroughs with derelict land capable of being renewed, no fewer than 42 authorities failed to deal with *any* acreage. At this rate – about 2,000 acres treated in England and Wales each year – it will take us more than fifty years to simply clear the official backlog of dereliction.

The Distribution of Blight

Dereliction is very unevenly distributed over the nation. Government figures for 1966 showed that 0·29 per cent of England was officially derelict, but in Lancashire, for instance, the figure was 0·95 of the county, while in Ince-in-Makerfield, Lancashire, some 37 per cent of the urban district was derelict. Perhaps the only surprising thing is that the county with the greatest dereliction – just over 16,000 acres – was not in the old industrial North, but Cornwall – principally the result of china-clay workings. The six counties of Cornwall, Lancashire, Durham, Staffordshire, the West Riding and Northumberland accounted for about 65 per cent of the total derelict land in England.* In Wales a third of the total was in the mining county of Glamorgan, which alone had more dereliction than the whole of the East Midlands region in England.

Apart from the obvious correlation between extensive wastelands and extensive mineral workings, it is significant that the most afflicted areas are far from Whitehall,

* A map of the blots of dereliction in any of these counties looks very like a Jackson Pollock painting, a thickly spattered canvas, though artlessly contrived.

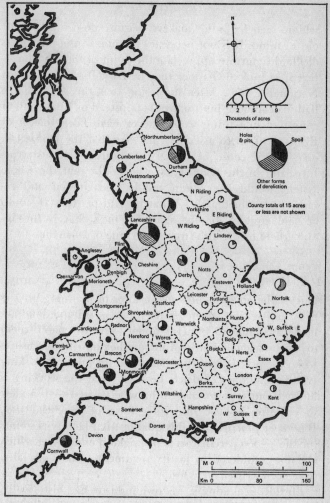

Derelict land in England and Wales, 1964. Acreage justifying treatment. Compiled from returns submitted by local authorities to the Ministry of Housing and Local Government and to the Secretary of State for Wales in response to Circular 55/64 (Reproduced by permission of the Controller of Her Majesty's Stationery Office. Crown Copyright).

seldom seen by policy makers, because unseen easily put out of mind. It is not necessary to endorse the principles of Plaid Cymru to appreciate the point of the Parliamentary speech of 26 October 1967 by Gwynfor Evans, Welsh Nationalist M.P. After supposing that the Aberfan tip had instead been built above Hampstead or Eton (and of course such a thing would never have been tolerated) Evans went on to assert: 'I am sure that the House can imagine the consequences in the industry and its structure, and in the State. I have no doubt that the whole system would have been totally re-examined and re-fashioned immediately.' What he said of Aberfan could be said equally for the shameful mess that is Ince-in-Makerfield or the filth-strewn coastline of Durham.

The Damagers

One of the government's major aims of planning powers is 'to ensure that the necessary rights in suitable land are made available to mineral undertakers to enable them to meet national needs'. But another aim is 'to ensure, wherever practicable, that land used for mineral working is not abandoned and left derelict when the working is finished but is restored or otherwise treated with a view to bringing it back into some form of beneficial use'. *Wherever practicable*: this qualification largely accounts for the 43,000 derelict acres in England and Wales which are not considered to justify treatment – that, officially, have been written off as lost.

Lord Robens admits, 'My own industry has, historically, been responsible for more disfigurement of the countryside than any other.' Even now a shrinking Coal Board holds about 300,000 acres; about a fifth of that is occupied by active pits, including spoil heaps, and more than half the total is designated agricultural land, but includes land which will be required for future extensions of collieries and for new spoil heaps. At the end of April 1968, the N C B still had 374 active pits (but 70 were to be closed in 1968–69) and about 170 million tons of coal are still being produced each year, all but 7 million tons by deep mining methods. Opencast mining disfigures large areas, but for a very much shorter period (on average three years) and the disfigured land is restored. Deep mines operate for decades and throw up a ton of waste for every three tons of marketable coal; about 1,000 acres a year are buried under colliery spoil and they are seldom reclaimed. In all, coal extraction affects at least 6,000 acres a year – in South Wales alone, according to the Council for the Protection of Rural Wales, about 100 acres of new land are buried by mine waste every year. Yet Lord Robens has said, 'We can no longer leave our litter around the countryside in the hope that the state will clear it up like a glorified dustman. None of the great industries can honestly say that it has yet done as much as it ought in meeting this obligation.' The coal industry least of all.

With the gradual decline of coal working – annual production is expected to fall to 120 million tons by 1975 – sand and gravel operators will soon exceed the N C B as the principal scar-makers. Production – now about 100 million tons a year – will, according to the Sand and Gravel Association of Great Britain, rise to 170 million by 1975, when it will be Britain's largest extractive industry. The South East Economic Planning Council estimates that in its region alone, 25,175 acres will be required for sand and gravel working between 1965 and 1972 and 21,925 acres between 1973 and 1977. The industry has a better record of land redemption than the coal industry, although the 1966–7 report of the Council for the

Preservation of Rural England said of sand and gravel operators: 'The industry has been its own worst enemy because, although a number of leading companies now take great care to prepare the land for re-use after exploitation, many others still do not.'

Quarrying of limestone, sandstone, chalk, slate and igneous rocks is proceeding at well over 90 million tons a year; these activities which, wrote John Oxenham, 'cut across the landscape like an open gash', he estimated to require some 800 acres a year. The 'Technology in Conservation' study group at the second Countryside in 1970 conference said that no restoration of limestone or slate quarries was being done, and it envisaged no new technical developments that would make restoration possible.*

The pits and spoil tips of china-clay workings in Cornwall sterilize a thirty-square-mile area around St Austell. Practically no restoration is done or appears even possible. Brick-clay production, in Bedfordshire and the Soke of Peterborough alone, now consumes more than 2,500 acres, growing by well over fifty acres a year. In the Oxford Clay belt near Bedford, more than 100,000 tons of clay are gouged out of the earth every week. Because of the scarcity of filling material, almost no reclamation is done. Gypsum, granite, salt, lead and tin production leave permanent scars, pollute rivers and subside land; little or no restoration is done by any of these industries. Ironstone production – which requires each year about 500 acres for an annual production of 16 million tons – is,

---

* But in the *Town Planning Review*, C. T. Crompton has argued that in Caernarvonshire, where 30,000 tons of slate is quarried each year, the waste could at least be cleaned up and the high, exposed scars near Rhyd-Ddu, which spoil views of Snowdon, could be softened.

along with opencast coal mining, an encouraging exception. As a result of the Ironstone Restoration Fund, set up in 1951, the gashes are progressively healed, the land restored for other uses.*

The Damage

Waste heaps on the earth are the most apparent by-products of this energetic exploitation of mineral resources. Collieries and china-clay workings produce the most spectacular and intractable eyesores. 'A slag heap † is at best a hideous thing, because it is so planless and functionless,' wrote George Orwell in *The Road to Wigan Pier*. 'It is something just dumped on the earth, like the emptying of a giant's dustbin.' About a third of the derelict acres in England, and well over half of those in Wales and Scotland, are made up of spoil heaps. 'These harsh black pyramids', as Trevor Thomas has called them, are most damaging to the environment: at once awesome and malevolent, they rise as high as 300 feet from the cramped floors of the South Wales valleys. A single tip contains five million or more tons of spoil; its lowering presence above a mining village is never deniable, blotting the sun.

In flatter places, colliery heaps (composed of poor quality coal, shale, dirt and stone) damage by their repetition as well as their bulk. They are truly what Ian Nairn, in another context, has called Things in Fields. Parts of

---

*Detailed discussion in Chapter 8.

†Technically, Orwell should have said *spoil* heap. Slag is the waste from, mainly, iron and steel manufacture, not coal extraction. The confusion is common. When John Cordle, M.P., unsuccessfully tabled a bill in Parliament in 1966 to remove spoil tips, he called it the Slagheaps Bill. In fact, slag is not a major problem; it is in demand for a variety of purposes and nearly all of it is sold.

Lancashire, spattered with spoil heaps, prompted J. B. Priestley in *English Journey* to write: 'The ugliness is so complete that it is almost exhilarating. It challenges you to live there.' In Durham and Northumberland, an aerial survey by the NCB has pinpointed 281 heaps. In the West Riding a county council survey has found more than 100 heaps, of which sixty-four are 'major physical features'. All but fifteen of them are active and growing each day. Nottinghamshire has 111 colliery heaps; some of them individually cover more than 100 acres.

Hundreds of acres of the central lowlands of Scotland are dotted with spent oil shale 'bings' as high as 200 feet, fan-shaped and flat-topped, many of them alight by spontaneous combustion. The burning bings pollute watercourses and emit toxic salts. 'Little is more likely to affect severely the psychological atmosphere of the Lothians growth area than the continued existence of these prominent eyesores,' according to the Lothians Regional Survey and Plan, 1966. Cement, pottery, glass and chemical works often throw up their rings of sometimes toxic mounds; electricity generating stations, gas works and boiler plants create their ash and clinker tips. The variety – of shape and size and content – of man's waste heaps is wondrous.

Holes in the ground, which account for about 30,000 acres of the official dereliction in England and Wales, are less apparent to the eye, though little less wasteful of land. The modern dragline excavators used in opencast coal mining can move 1,400 tons of material an hour and seek out coal seams 500 feet down. In the Bedfordshire brickfield, massive 'walking' excavators (they waddle rather than walk) dig to depths of 100 feet, producing the immense pits known in the trade as 'knotholes', the floors rippled with manmade hills and dales. The existing holes in Bedfordshire would require as much filling material as would fill St Paul's Cathedral 275 times.

By such standards, the pockets in hillsides from quarrying and the wet or dry pits made by sand and gravel digging seem relatively minor disfigurements. But they are widely distributed. Near London in the Lee Valley alone, the Civic Trust has found, over an area of 6,000 acres, 'a wilderness of gravel digging and its legacy of pits and derelict machinery'. As the main reserves of gravel near London become largely worked out – and this will happen by the early 1970s – areas farther from the capital can expect similar scenes of desolation.

Holes *and* heaps in juxtaposition are features of some industries, or of a variety of industries operating in a restricted space. Holes and heaps of every imaginable, bizarre configuration blight hundreds of acres in the Lower Swansea Valley, the legacy of hundreds of years of coal mining, copper working, lead, zinc and tinplate production. The pits and waste-mountains of the china-clay district of Cornwall constitute what in the past has often been called 'a lunar landscape'. The St Austell landscape is pocked by steep-sided pits 150 to 200 feet deep, each covering eight to ten acres, and because for each ton of marketable china clay about six to eight tons of quartz and sand waste is produced, a range of conical or tubular tips, each on average 150 feet high and occupying three acres, excel the pits in assaulting the eye.

The layman's first question, where man has made holes and heaps side by side, is why not simply push the 'eaps into the 'oles. Sometimes this can be done, and it could be done more often than it is, but in the china-clay fields it is largely prevented by the immense cost of the earth-moving and because the depths of usable clay are not known and so far few if any pits have been 'bottomed'.

So long as there may be profits buried at still lower depths, the owners will not tolerate any notions of shoving their own mess into their own holes.

Man's Other Wastelands

Seldom officially derelict, but no less defacements of the landscape, are hundreds of thousands of other acres degraded by man. In the D. H. Lawrence country near Nottingham, packed into one obscene square mile, are derelict sewage works, abandoned colliery buildings, rusting railway tracks, a crumbling viaduct, and – almost inevitable accretions to such areas – the grotesque mess of itinerant scrap merchants. Amidst the shameful scene are sprinkled slum houses still occupied by those who can afford nothing better. It is a scene repeated countless times in countless places in the old and tired industrial parts of Britain, marred by the freakish hardware left behind when man has moved on. Nor are such scenes always the result of man's past actions: working industry, so often improperly controlled and contemptuous of its environment, frequently throws up messes hardly distinguishable from those of abandoned industrial sites.

Military lands – or former military lands – can rival industrial dereliction in their sterilization of ground and disfigurement of the countryside. Today the Ministry of Defence holds about 600,000 acres in Britain. The ministry does not consider that any of this land is derelict – large chunks of it may look so, but it is being held against some possible future emergency or other military requirements. 'We retain a number of inactive camps and airfields as reserves but we try to maintain these to such a state that they could be reactivated in a short time,' says the ministry. 'Additionally, cases sometimes arise where some buildings on our own land are no longer required as such but where we wish to retain the land. In those cases, we try to prevent the redundant buildings from becoming unsightly or to demolish them when money is available.'

In many of the 350,000 acres used by the Services for training, there is a barbaric desolation created by tanks and guns. Imber Village on Salisbury Plain has been almost totally destroyed by practice shelling; only the deteriorating church of St Giles, with a halo of barbed wire, remains. On Dartmoor (in a National Park!) the Army's heavy vehicles are tearing up some 30,000 acres, prehistoric earthworks and tumuli are destroyed, and the moor is sprayed with missiles, often unexploded and just lying about. At Lulworth in Dorset the 120mm. guns of Chieftain tanks batter $5\frac{1}{2}$ miles of some of the most splendid shoreline in England – and the Services occupy another 185 miles of coastline and estuarial shores in Britain which they can mistreat at will. Within the Lulworth range the old village of Tyneham has been reduced to rubble. Vast acres for military training are obviously essential ('in the national interest') but the examples illustrate how dereliction can be concocted by the Services and raise the question whether all this dereliction is essential to maintain the nation's military security.

More often the military junk littering the landscape is on property which the Ministry of Defence has released to private owners, who in turn have failed to clean up the eyesores. Since 1945 the ministry has shed nearly 11 million acres requisitioned during the war; between 1962 and 1967 it disposed of 130,000 acres; in 1968, it was disposing of 26,000 more acres. The ministry says that when selling surplus land it tries to get the new owners to keep the buildings from becoming derelict, or to demolish them to ground level, but 'we are sometimes disappointed by the result'. This is the case with the 'gun emplacements, searchlight holders, assorted brick and concrete buildings and ugly twists of barbed wire' – as *The Times* described them – which still remain as wartime relics atop the White Cliffs of Dover, an area of 'outstanding natural beauty'.

In 1960 Colonel D. E. Newton estimated that there were probably about 100 airfields then lying derelict in the country. Most of them had then or have since been sold to private buyers, the ministry handing over the land uncleared and compensating the buyer for those areas occupied by hard standings and buildings. But the buyers – usually farmers – commonly just strip the buildings of anything saleable and then leave them to disintegrate slowly; they spend the compensation not on clearing but to buy a tractor. If there is a nearby demand by road constructors for the concrete in the runways, the owner may clear them. More frequently he just farms around them, the land under concrete both unattractive and lost permanently to agriculture.*

With the sharp reduction in track mileage started at

---

*A much more serious agricultural problem, though outside the scope of this book, is the derelict land created by man's shortsighted exploitation of the soil and contempt for nature's ecological balance. Garth Christian wrote of 'those two million acres of bracken-infested "wet desert" in northern Britain where the natural processes of soil development have been reversed by centuries of burning and over-grazing'. Wholesale removal of trees and hedgerows is causing wind erosion in areas such as the Fens. The destruction of natural wind breaks (which are also habitats for the wild life essential for the balance of nature) has resulted in Lincolnshire in seeds being blown away as soon as they have been planted. These misuses of the earth's surface are extremely dangerous. As Christian reminded us: 'Two inches of topsoil may be the creation of a thousand years.'

British Rail during the Beeching era, disused rail lines – along with abandoned stations, signal boxes, sheds and bridges – have created in the 1960s a new kind of dereliction. In the West Riding alone there are now 2,000 miles of disused railways; and in Norfolk, according to the East Anglia Economic Planning Council, 1,000 of the county's 2,451 derelict acres are the result of abandoned railways. As David Gibson-Watt, M.P., puts it: 'Land which becomes derelict as the result of the closure of railways is in a slightly different category than land left derelict as a result of industrial activity because it threads its way through so much other unspoilt land.' This is often true, and the land devoured by a railway line is not as light as may be imagined: on average, one mile of line covers ten acres.

Although the British Railways Board is still one of the largest landowners in the country, with some 250,000 acres, in the twenty years up to 31 December 1967 the board closed 6,400 miles of line and sold 1,900 miles. Including all land and buildings as well as the lines themselves, the board disposed of 17,500 acres between 1964 and 1967. British Rail says that it tries to keep the time between a closure and the beginning of another use to a minimum and 'if the land cannot be put to another use immediately, every effort is made to prevent its becoming a danger, a nuisance or an eyesore. If lines cannot be sold they are regularly inspected and any necessary maintenance and renewals are carried out; scrub is cleared, and pest, vermin and weeds controlled.' However, anyone who has noticed the state of some closed rural lines, the deteriorating jumble of Victorian buildings clustered round an erstwhile stop, may question whether British Rail is always as scrupulously amenity-conscious as that. And there is no guarantee that the purchaser of British Rail property – in rural areas, almost always the farmer whose holdings adjoin the railway – will not permit the eyesores to remain. He will probably shove the embankments into the cuttings and return the acreage taken by the line to agriculture; but the miscellaneous buildings may well end up as yet more examples of the unsightly 'agricultural architecture' which so often blots the countryside. In urban areas, when British Rail sells surplus land, market forces come into play and there are better prospects of complete reclamation to new uses.

The waterways which once served commerce but have now been abandoned present special problems, whether of restoration to pleasure-waterways or in-filling to remove eyesores and regain the land for farming or other uses. An unused, unmaintained canal can be a very unpleasant strip of dereliction, a swimming bath for vermin, a dumping ground for discarded domestic hardware, a tempting place for industry's polluting wastes. Amongst its embarrassing riches of dereliction, the Lower Swansea Valley can also count unused and unpleasantly polluted waterways. So can many other outworn industrial areas.

On nationalization in 1948, the British Waterways Board took over about 2,000 miles of waterways, including some lengths already abandoned or closed to navigation: about 1,400 miles are now open to navigation. It costs between £200 and £300 simply to maintain one mile of disused canal, and in 1965 the board estimated that it cost £6,000 a mile to eliminate a narrow rural canal and £9,000 a mile for a wide rural canal, 'designed broadly to re-create pre-canal conditions'. According to the Ministry of Transport, 'Whatever is done with them, the non-commercial waterways will cost the taxpayer £600,000 a year, and to keep open for pleasure-cruising all the non-commercial waterways now available for that purpose would cost a further £340,000.' (At 1965 prices.) The brutal economics of this situation suggest that if anything the mileage of derelict waterways is liable to increase.

The Possibilities

Heaps and holes, industrial junklands, abandoned military lands, railways and waterways – for nearly all these dead lands there are new lives . . . given the money, the national will to do the job, and greater injections of imagination than have so far characterized our puny efforts at land renewal. Very few of the lands lost by man's works cannot be recovered by man's technology and ingenuity.

Hugo Young has pointed out: 'If all the land in England now officially called derelict were restored, its area could accommodate at normal density no fewer than a million homes. Thus it could replace the need for overspill and the invasion of green land for at least five years. Alternatively, it could provide 45,000 playing fields or 90,000 acres of park.' Though a journalistic simplification, this translation of spoiled land into houses or playing fields underlines how wasteful is our industrial dereliction.

Heaps can be levelled and returned to agriculture (sometimes without even the addition of topsoil) or turned into industrial estates; they can be contoured and planted to become green space. It is the very urban areas now ringed by spoil tips which most frequently lack the 'lung' of nearby open space. Even presently derelict acres – which for all their ugliness have the virtues of open air and elbow room – are often used to a surprising extent for leisure. In Lancashire people picnic beneath the shade of shale heaps; in Nottinghamshire men race whippets on the man-made mountains; in the Swansea Valley anglers spend their Sundays bent over miserable flashes. People deserve better places for their pleasures.

Many heaps need not involve any earth-moving to become attractive landscape features. Compared to other European nations, Britain is deficient in woodlands: only about seven per cent of our land area is occupied by trees. The average in Continental countries is two to three times higher; even West Germany – with a population and an area very similar to Britain's – is wooded over twenty-nine per cent of its surface. There are technical problems in planting trees straight into shale heaps, but they are by no means insurmountable. According to the Forestry Commission, 'It has been proved for a decade or more that spoil heaps are usually potentially fertile, provide sufficient moisture to support tree growth, there are seldom excessive erosion and instability difficulties, and toxicity is rare.' Corsican and Lodgepole pines, birch and grey alder, sycamore, beech and cherry, and a dozen other species will usually grow happily in shale. Where full reclamation is uneconomic, painting pit heaps green with grass and trees is the cheap answer and can transform an eyesore into a pleasant landscape twenty times faster than by leaving nature to do the job.

Trees on spoil heaps in the Welsh valleys have been suggested by the Council for Nature on grounds of safety. The Council has studied the 'ban-forests' in the Alpine villages of Switzerland, broad belts of trees rising behind the villages and reducing exposure to avalanches of snow, landslips and falls of stone. The council's suggestion was prompted by Aberfan. 'The costs of land acquisition, planting and management would be less than those of removing the millions of tons of unstable spoil which could never be entirely safe on hills subject to heavy rain and other erosive forces,' argues the council. 'Without damage to their essentially protective role the forests could be managed to produce an economic return. There could also be another return in the form of renewed confidence to valleys which have experienced so much of the unrelieved effects of the extractive processes in a deteriorating environment.'

Holes in the ground offer many possibilities of after-use. Dry sand and gravel pits and worked out clay and chalk pits can be restored to new purposes by filling with builders' rubble, pulverized power-station ash, or town refuse. Strictly controlled tipping of refuse (particularly if it is first pulverized) into dry pits does not only in time, as John Stephenson has said, achieve 'virtual miracles ... playing fields, sports stadia and parks', but provides a constructive solution to man's growing problem of where to dispose of his ever-increasing mountains of waste. More than 14 million tons of house and trade refuse is now collected in England and Wales every year. This means about one ton a year from every dwelling. Frank Flintoff, assistant director of public health engineering for the Greater London Council, forecasts: 'The volume of refuse to be disposed of between 1970 and 1990 will probably equal the whole of that disposed of from 1900 to 1970.'

John Oxenham has suggested that near resort areas, worked-out dry excavations could be converted into pleasant and visually unobtrusive caravan or camping sites at low cost; near urban areas, they could sometimes be turned into amphitheatres, race tracks or adventure playgrounds. Newcastle University planners have suggested that sometimes disused quarries might be ideal sites for ugly gas-holders – nicely out of view.

Worked-out wet pits could be used for fish-rearing, could sometimes be incorporated in water conservation or purification schemes, and very often can be turned over to recreational uses. Indeed, around London this is already happening to such an extent that the demand by water sports clubs for wet gravel pits exceeds the supply. A survey in November 1967 by the regional sports councils in the South East of fifty-six wet gravel pits in west London found 'intensive use' of all of them, supporting sixty-six sailing and angling clubs with a combined membership of nearly 10,000 persons. Wet pits too small or otherwise unsuitable for recreation can, with a little tidying up, become excellent sites for nature study – and refuges for wild life. Peter Scott, on the B B C television programme *Look*, has demonstrated how great is the variety and density of wild life in the disused ball clay pits of Devon.

The heaps and holes of dereliction could in many cases be transformed into the 'country parks' proposed in the new Countryside Act. The government's white paper, *Leisure in the Countryside*, referred to the growing traffic congestion from leisure-seekers converging on seaside or inland beauty spots: 'Other areas might do just as well, and might be easier to reach.' Reclaimed derelict land near urban areas could often meet this need, particularly for the small picnic places proposed – 'an acre or so of land and space for parking cars ... something better than a lay-by'. Disused railways can sometimes be turned into long-distance footpaths or cycle routes.* Abandoned canals can sometimes be restored for pleasure cruising (as has been done with the Monmouthshire Canal) and the fees in time pay for the restoration.

Where pressures on land are urgent, reclamation is

---

*There are difficulties. The Ramblers' Association points out that where considerable sections of tracks are in cuttings, they are not really suitable for long walks.

done. For example, between 1946 and 1963 in the West Midlands 9,000 acres of dereliction were cleared for housing, new industry and recreational space. But where the pressures on land seem less urgent – as in many parts of the North and in Wales – reclamation is too seldom done: it *appears* not to pay.

Certainly there are obstacles – some real, some imagined, most of them a matter of our attitudes towards dereliction rather than any insurmountable financial or administrative or technical obstructions. And nearly all the supposed obstacles are exaggerated. What is really stopping us?

Chapter 3: The Obstacles

It seems a curious paradox that a nation so quick and generous in opening its purse strings for charity to the afflicted of every nation, should be so hesitant, apathetic and almost resistant to suggestions for helping its own districts and its own land, where these have been damaged in contributing to the national prosperity.

– JOHN OXENHAM, former adviser on land reclamation to the Ministry of Housing and Local Government

THE renewal of derelict land does not fit comfortably into the British way of doing things. It is not a subject properly approached by that cherished committee method which results in consensus and compromise. Something bolder is called for. Too much of the too little land renewal already done – and done on an *ad hoc* basis – has been a compromise between doing nothing at all and doing the job properly. The results, for the sake of immediate economies, have been too often piecemeal, timid and unimaginative. Dullness has replaced dereliction.

Sometimes it has been the fault of central government, questioning every detail of a local authority's reclamation scheme, whittling off pennies here and there, granting funds only when a scheme has been sadly truncated. Sometimes it has been the fault of local authorities, penny-pinching by the council, a failure to consult landscape architects, a lack of imagination and drive so common in the depressed areas of dereliction. Compromised reclamation projects are the result of the consensus-committee approach which, it must be said, is exceptionally efficient at one thing: extracting and sometimes inventing all possible obstacles to action. Inaction is thus intellectually vindicated.

Money Troubles

Apart from a lack of real determination to clear up dereliction and a failure to recognize that beauty is priceless, money is nonetheless a major obstacle. The average cost of reclamation schemes submitted by local authorities since the war to the government for grant has been about £550 an acre (excluding the cost of the land) or £1,100 an acre (including acquisition). If no more than a cosmetic treatment is the aim, it has been found in Durham and elsewhere that afforestation of derelict land can be achieved at costs below £200 an acre, including the price of overseeing the trees until they are fully established – about five years. In Lancashire the gross costs of reclamation schemes completed between 1954 and 1966 ranged from £78 an acre (including acquisition, engineering works and cultivation) to as much as £644 an acre. The average per acre costs of acquisition, including fees, was £67; of engineering works £211; of cultivation £31 – £309 for everything. And with three of Lancashire's thirteen completed schemes, the redeemed land was resold at a profit – in one case for twice the total price of the reclamation.

Despite the aid (sometimes) of government grants, many local authorities are loath to spend even this much. They argue – as the Countryside in 1970 conference noted – 'that dereliction is the price which has been paid for the past prosperity of the nation as a whole and that putting it right is a national and not a local responsibility'. Many local authorities – even when government grants are forthcoming – simply can't afford to spend even this much.

For the fact that dereliction is usually at once a contributing cause of decline and depression and one of the results of decline and depression means that large concentrations of derelict land tend to be features of poor areas. Reclamation falls on those local authorities least able to afford it and which lack the staff and expertise to do the job.

For example, until the formation of a derelict-land unit in the Welsh Office immediately after the Aberfan tragedy, practically no reclamation had been done in Wales. This is not surprising in view of the farcical local government structure in the principality: 164 non-county boroughs and urban districts, forty-three of them with a population below 5,000 and a penny rate product of less than £600. Some Welsh authorities realize less than £250 on a penny (and similar situations exist in the depressed areas of England and Scotland). In consequence nothing gets done except when the Welsh Office holds out the carrot of reclamation grants and its derelict-land unit goes to the local authorities, offering its expertise and chivvying them into action.*

Small and poor local authorities, if in government-designated development areas, may qualify for an eighty-five per cent grant under the Industrial Development Act 1966 towards reclamation, providing the proposed schemes meet the Board of Trade condition that they will contribute towards the development of industry in the area. Poor authorities also qualify for a rate deficiency

---

*The *Western Mail* does not consider that this happens often enough. The paper has accused the Welsh Office of sluggishness in clearing and improving the appearance of Welsh mine tips: 'There appears to be no Welsh Office supervision or policy.'

grant, which can bring central government assistance up to about ninety-five per cent. Yet with their inevitable pre-occupation in keeping their rates down and with more urgent calls on their small resources – housing, schools, essential services – even the five per cent is often hard to find. In a letter to the Prime Minister in January 1968, the Chairman of the Northern Economic Planning Council, T. Dan Smith, made precisely that point and urged the government to increase the grant in development areas to 100 per cent. The letter was passed on to Anthony Green-wood, the Minister of Housing, and nothing has happened. The government fears that a 100 per cent grant would en-courage wastefulness; local authorities would have no stimulus to keep the costs of reclamation schemes to a minimum.

Local authorities with derelict land within a national park or an (otherwise) area of outstanding natural beauty can apply for a 75 per cent grant towards reclamation under the National Parks and Access to the Countryside Act 1949.* But instances of industrial dereliction in beauty spots are naturally relatively infrequent. The pro-blem in such areas is usually the active winning of clay, sand or potash to which restoration conditions are attached and no grant is available.

Since April 1967 all areas of the country have qualified under the Local Government Act 1966 for reclamation grants up to 50 per cent. Schemes in development areas which do not meet the Board of Trade's requirements for the 85 per cent grant may also be approved under this legislation. But until April 1968 – because of the

---

* As amended by the Local Authorities (Land) Act 1963, authorities can carry out works of reclamation on land not in their ownership, providing they get the consent of all persons having an interest in the land.

government's refusal, as part of the credit squeeze, to consider grants for amenity schemes – the 50 per cent grant was not widely available, since a majority of reclamation schemes are designed simply to create pleasant green open space.* And, as we have seen, the government is not even now actually encouraging applications for amenity schemes. In any event – particularly in the 'grey' areas of northern England which, though depressed, are not included in the development areas – the 50 per cent grant is clearly an inadequate incentive.

Even so, by September 1968 the Ministry of Housing and Local Government had since 1960 approved 152 reclamation or landscaping schemes in England, covering 2,565 acres. About £640,000 had by then been paid in grants; the total estimated cost of the approved schemes was about £2.5 million. The Welsh Office had approved about £1 million in grants for 30 schemes. While these totals are encouraging, they are nowhere near sufficient and affect a mere fraction of the total derelict acreage.

In general, the Minister of Housing (who administers all these grants, sometimes with the advice of the Board of Trade) will consider schemes if he is 'satisfied that the land is derelict [i.e. not in active use for any purpose] and that the works proposed are requisite to enable the land to be brought into use or improved in appearance at a reasonable cost'. He will not approve for grants 'works which would normally be undertaken in the course of the development of the land, or for the purpose of putting it to use after reclamation has been undertaken'. This means that there are no grants for the construction of roads and sewers, erection of buildings or the laying out of gardens or sports fields.

* Thus, in 1967, Lancashire was able to landscape only 13 derelict acres, and its 1968 programme was severely cut back or delayed.

The problem of 'after-value' also discourages many local authorities from applying for these grants. If after reclamation the land approved for grant is to be retained by the local authority for amenity purposes, the government does not subtract any after-value from its grant – there isn't any after-value, in terms that can be conveniently quantified. The ministry states:

However, if the redeemed land is to be sold or leased or appropriated for development or for agricultural or horticultural use the capital value of the land for the intended use will be set off against the expenditure eligible for grant. The value will be the disposal price or the estimated capital value of the land for the purpose for which it is to be used as determined by the district valuer.

But as T. Dan Smith has argued, the current practice of deducting after-value from grants adds to the financial difficulties of local authorities 'as some time might elapse before land is disposed of and after-value realized'. He has urged that in all cases the grant should be paid in full and the after-value refunded to the government when the land is disposed of or developed.

Forestry Commission woodland grants are occasionally available at £22 12s. per acre for amenity schemes on derelict land *if* it can be shown that timber production is also a major objective. But this is not often the case.* While trees grow adequately enough in spoil tips and dry excavations, such sites are seldom suitable for intensive production of first-class timber. 'Derelict land is nearly always a poor timber-production prospect for one technical reason or another – smoke pollution, unstable ground, extreme exposure, bad drainage, liability to

*Though Durham, with Forestry Commission grants, has planted large acreages for a total cost of about £50 an acre.

vandalism, or severe chemical pollution of the ground,' says a Forestry Commission spokesman. 'We have acquired several such sites in the past, but now avoid them unless, for example, they adjoin an existing forest and are better than average.' The commission's general line on derelict land reclamation is that 'it is a "social cost" to be borne by the ratepayers – not an "uneconomic cost" to be set against timber growing.'

Administrative Messes

Britain's local government structure, with nearly 2,000 separate administrative units, is itself an obstacle to land reclamation – as it is to numerous functions and actions both more and less vital. The Royal Commissions on Local Government in England and in Scotland, appointed in 1966, are to recommend a less administratively chaotic structure and will certainly urge a severe reduction in the number of authorities. But their recommendations will not begin to be enforced until 1972 at the earliest, and it is safe to assume that only those recommendations politically advantageous to the party in power at Westminster will be enforced anyway. Wales has already taken the first step towards a rationalization: *Local Government in Wales* (July 1967) urged eventual reduction to five counties and thirty-six smaller districts. In the meantime – and it may be a long time – the Countryside in 1970's complaint holds true: 'The large number of local authorities who may be involved in any planned scheme of reclamation can undoubtedly make co-ordination of effort difficult in some cases.'

Consider, for example, Lancashire, where there are nearly as many holes in the administrative county (eighteen autonomous county boroughs and 109 county districts) as there are in Lancashire's 2,481 acres of derelict pitlands. The problems of co-ordination that this administratively mad pattern presents make it all the more remarkable that Lancashire has managed to lead the nation in land renewal. Proof perhaps that determination can overcome even the obstacles of an administrative Wonderland.

The multiplicity of authorities, many very small, means also that their capabilities and their approaches (if any) to the problem of dereliction vary wildly. Many authorities are simply not applying for the financial assistance – though still inadequate – which *is* available. As the Department of Economic Affairs study *The North West* said: 'Finance is not the only obstacle to more rapid progress ... some of the dereliction in the region could be treated at quite a modest cost, but some local authorities seem to lack a sense of urgency in dealing with dereliction in their areas.' Also, because of ineffectual officers and councillors or lingering muck=money beliefs, many authorities do not adequately control the now-working industries which are making tomorrow's dereliction. They impose timid, woolly restoration conditions on mineral extractors; they fail to ensure that the conditions imposed are obeyed. Or because of the General Development Order they simply can't impose any controls.

Nor is central government guiltless in this respect. On occasions the Minister of Housing 'calls in' planning applications by mineral operators and then lays down the restoration conditions. Lax ministry conditions account for some forty acres of dereliction in Nottinghamshire by gypsum extractors. Ambiguous ministry conditions permit the brick-makers in the Oxford Clay belt to profit from the dereliction they create. A typical ministry condition begins: 'Overburden with any other suitable filling materials available at reasonable times *on reasonable terms* [my italics] shall be deposited within the excavated areas. ...' Because of this fuzzy terminology, the brickmakers have construed 'on reasonable terms' to mean not that they should not have to pay an inordinate price to obtain filling material, but that anyone who tips filling material into their pits for them must pay – but not an inordinate price!

These bungles by planners are part of a cumbersome administrative machinery for land renewal at both national and local levels. T. Dan Smith has rightly argued: 'If reclamation is to be speeded up ... administrative procedures involved in authorizing grants need to be streamlined, work delegated from Whitehall to regional offices of the Ministry of Housing and Local Government.' He called for 'greater flexibility' in administering grants. John Casson has suggested that the government give block grants 'and trust local authorities * to use them wisely instead of dogging one's steps at every stage of every scheme and causing the delays that have characterized past efforts in the fields of reclamation, landscaping and recreation'. The ministry's decision in April 1968 to allow its regional offices to pass judgement on applications for grants for all reclamation schemes below £150,000 should go some way towards meeting these complaints, as should its decision to invite three-year, rather than year-to-year, reclamation projects from local authorities.

---

*It is, however, true that very occasionally local authorities are over-ambitious or even try things on with the ministry. One recent and unreasonably dear reclamation scheme submitted to the ministry envisaged the planting of exotic and expensive trees from Kew Gardens. The local authority was advised to do with more modest vegetation.

At the local level, the biggest administrative obstacle is frequently the acquisition of derelict land.* Landowners (including too often the N C B) hang on in the hope of eventually making money from selling the shale in spoil tips, or they hang on in the hope of forcing the local authority to finally, in exasperation, pay an inflated price. A. Latham, Derbyshire's planning officer, considers the main bottlenecks to land reclamation to be valuation and acquisition: 'The site may have some small value, for example most waste materials can find a market over a period, so that the owner may wish to retain it or demand a price which is uneconomic having regard to the restoration work needed.'

Sometimes owners are simply bloody-minded, unwilling either to improve the derelict land themselves or to sell it for improvement. The multiplicity of landowners in areas of concentrated dereliction, such as the Lower Swansea Valley,† sometimes cause delay and complications. And the reluctance of so many local authorities to use compulsory purchase orders simply for reclamation also creates delays and encourages owners to hold out for a higher price. As Lancashire's chief planner, Aylmer Coates, puts it: 'Because the County Council is loath to use compulsory purchase orders, land that cost us £10–£20 an acre at the beginning is now costing £800 – and for the dirtiest land in Europe!'

* Of course this is a problem with *all* land, but as the Countryside in 1970 conference recommended, more generous grants would at least 'encourage local authorities to buy up derelict land sufficiently in advance of reclamation to avoid work being held up by the process of acquisition'.

† There a major problem was that the landowners looked for the industrial-use prices and the local authority for the derelict-land prices and the gap could not easily be bridged.

Technical Problems

Many of the so-called technical obstacles to land renewal are imaginary. Before the war, reclamation required armies of men with picks and shovels and there had been little research into growing vegetation on spoiled earth. Since the war, planners need no longer stand intimidated beneath gigantic tips and scratch their heads: the equipment now exists to do what Michael Graham has called 'Mahomet-like moving of landscapes by machines'. With modern earth-moving machines the down-to-earth job of reclamation is the least of many problems. John Oxenham's useful guide to reclamation techniques describes this formidable modern equipment: scrapers that move 300 cubic yards of earth a minute, graders that lift a ton of spoil every second, excavators that strip 1,500 tons of hard ground or soft rock in twelve hours. In opencast mining, the Coal Board now uses draglines with buckets large enough to hold a motor car comfortably and which can move 1,400 tons of material per hour.

The technical revolution includes tree transplanters. The Michigan Tree Transplanter, designed in America and used here by the Civic Trust and the NCB for moving semi-mature trees, is a sixteen-ton monster capable of lifting and carrying without damage trees up to sixty feet high and weighing as much as seven tons. The mortality rate after transplanting has been less than ten per cent. Such machinery has led Lord Robens to declare confidently: 'If there is any coal under Dunsinane I am sure we will be able to transplant Birnam Wood to cover our tracks.'

The recent development of hydraulic seeding has made it possible literally to spray vegetation on the most intractable surfaces. A mulch of grass- and tree-seeds, fertilizers, chopped straw and water is sprayed under pressure over the raw surface, with very successful results. Selective weedkillers, species of short-growing grasses, and grass-growth regulators have been developed in recent years to reduce weeds and tall grasses and eliminate many of the problems of after-management.

Research by the British Ecological Society, by the botanists involved in the Lower Swansea Valley Project, and by numerous other universities and government bodies * have led to dramatic advances in soil making and have also proved conclusively that a wide range of flora will grow in inhospitable earth. Studies at Birmingham and Leeds Universities on growing plants in power-station ash have found that yields of rye grown in pulverized ash are sometimes superior to yields from conventional soil and that ash is superior to many soils in water-retaining capacity. Professor S. H. Beaver found that gravel, ironstone, sand and (sometimes) clay pits reclaimed for farming can have definite advantages: 'The lowering of the ground level may sometimes, by bringing the cultivable surface nearer to the water table, actually improve agriculture.' Studies by the National Agricultural Advisory Service, based on practical experience in returning opencast mining sites to farming, have revealed a number of technical problems, but with care in management, more fertilizers and heavier seed rates than on undisturbed land, the problems can be overcome. On 'flashy' derelict sites there are also problems of drainage; to overcome them adds to the costs of reclamation.

The real technical difficulties are either those of location – the heaps are uneconomically distant from the

* Including Glasgow, Newcastle, York and Edinburgh Universities; the Ministry of Agriculture, Forestry Commission and Nature Conservancy.

holes into which they might be pushed – or of the nature
of the extractive operation. Sometimes any pits available
in the vicinity of waste heaps are too shallow or there are
no adequate roads to them. Sometimes, however, it is just
a matter of planners failing to co-ordinate tipping and
extracting operations – or even plain inaction. Near
Stoke-on-Trent, for example, the landscape is punctuated
by deep conical marlholes and towering conical spoil tips
side by side – no doubt there are some 'technical problems' that prevent the too obvious solution to this natural
jigsaw.

The time-span of some mineral operations and the
absence of filling material for pits are genuine problems.
Because of the fluctuation in commodity prices, it is common for many china-clay workings to be left idle for
years in the hope of higher prices again, at which time the
workings resume. Local authorities often grant permission to contractors to remove saleable shale from coal
tips; but, because of fluctuating prices and demand or
because he lacks sufficient heavy equipment and manpower, the contractor works so slowly that the heaps are
eyesores for years.* The cement industry considers that
sixty years is the normal period in which to establish and
amortize the capital equipment required in any new
mineral undertaking, and the Minister of Housing has
often granted mineral extractors consents for 100 years or
more.

While opencast coal and ironstone sites are relatively
easy to restore – because they work comparatively thin
seams under a thick overburden and so the waste almost

---

* Though this practice can contribute to reducing the bulk of
waste tips and so apparently assist reclamation, it does not always do
so. The contractor gouges out the best and most accessible bits and
leaves the more intractable. The result is a worse mess than before.

equals the capacity of the holes – the working of sand, gravel and clay involves thick deposits below relatively thin overburden and there is little left over for infilling – even if the operator is scrupulous enough to retain the overburden for later restoration. Robin Best has estimated the restoration possibilities of brick-clay pits as fifteen per cent, of ball- and china-clay pits as nil.

The heaps as well as the holes of some mineral industries are so large that they present some technical difficulties. Deep-mined coal brings up on average a ton of waste for every five tons of saleable coal, and finding holes for such heaps or even flattening and contouring them, if sufficient adjacent land is not available, can be a real problem.* Also, ironically, colliery modernization exacerbates the waste problem. Nottinghamshire's chief planner, Jack Lowe, notes: 'The increase in mechanization and the exhaustion of the thicker, higher quality seams have resulted in an alarming increase in the quantities of colliery waste.' The situation with slate quarrying is even worse: the Rees Committee on the Welsh slate industry said in 1946, and it is still true, that to produce a ton of slate up to twenty tons or more of waste is produced, hurled down in finger-like heaps extending hundreds of yards from the slate workings.

---

*The Clean Air Act 1956 has resulted in larger areas of land being covered by spoil heaps, by requiring the N C B to take all practicable means of preventing spontaneous combustion in the tips. The practical result has been fewer high conical tips, which are more likely to combust, and more low flat tips which, while they may be more acceptable to the eye – particularly if expertly contoured by a landscape architect to fit the surrounding environment – obviously occupy more space.

A Matter of Attitudes

The North West Economic Planning Council has said: 'Extreme poverty has gone, but the habits it formed are still with us. The problem, therefore, is one of overcoming indifference.' Dereliction breeds resignation, an attitude of 'What was good enough for my father and for me is good enough for my children.' In the most despoiled districts of Nottinghamshire, Jack Lowe has detected 'a feeling of helplessness among the people ... the feeling that though man made the tips he cannot dismantle them'.

In time, apathy towards the environment can spawn yet more dangerous attitudes: these become entrenched and, even more than apathy, are deterrents to land renewal. Derek Senior, who wrote large parts of the Civic Trust's booklet *Derelict Land*, noted that the grim desolation of derelict areas 'dulls the spirit' and 'engenders a "derelict land mentality" that can never be eradicated until the mess itself has been cleared up. Dereliction, indeed, breeds a brutish insensibility, bordering on positive antagonism, to the life and loveliness of the natural landscape it has supplanted.'

In the mutilated valleys of South Wales and the scarred landscape of the North it is not uncommon to encounter positive hostility towards proposals for cleaning up the land. Older people particularly are proud and they are stubborn: they resent an outsider announcing that they live and always have lived in a debased environment; they have a peculiar conceit, even arrogance or possessiveness, about the industrial ugliness left by their forefathers. Maybe even love. In *The Other England*, Geoffrey Moorhouse wrote: 'In Lancashire, it seems, they prefer to acknowledge the dirt as a necessary coating to

the real values of life which lie beneath it. You're mucky
but I love you is the local philosophy, and making the
best of things as they are has been developed to a fine art.'
The mess is a symbol of their past energy and prosperity
and its very-hideousness today curiously binds the community together, creates a kind of blitz mentality. Aylmer
Coates has found in Lancashire what he calls 'a dereliction
neurosis', a tenacious attitude of 'let's stick together in
adversity'.

When William Mather took over the chairmanship of
the North West Economic Planning Council in April
1968, the first thing he said was: 'The problem of environment is the crucial one and that is where we must
start. If you are dirty and scruffy you lack self-confidence
and that is what has gone wrong with us.' Compare that
to a letter to the editor in a Rochdale newspaper: 'We
became black by determination and hard work. Time-
encrusted grime is part of us in the North of England and
should stay with us.'

The Missing Blueprints

Even if financial, administrative and technical problems
are overcome, even if attitudes of apathy or hostility are
erased, one major obstacle often remains: a real blueprint for action is missing. The government now invites,
but does not require, local authorities to draw up long-
term action plans for reclamation or improvement of
derelict land. But such plans require expertise, determination, and real commitment to land redemption – and
these are sparse qualities. The research which is essential
is not an art natural to most local authorities. Nor is the
resolution to prevent a bold plan from dilution by compromise. Nor is the sense of urgency to action that must

inhabit even the most patiently and thoroughly drawn-up blueprint. The bookshelves of planners' offices all over Britain are filled with action plans crippled by appeasement, getting daily dustier from a failure of will or follow-through.

Happily there are some exceptions. Lancashire, the West Riding, and County Durham in England and the Lothians in Scotland are among those who have not only produced carefully researched and reasoned blueprints for land renewal but are going ahead. But none of their plans matches in detail, imaginativeness and persuasiveness the five-year research project undertaken in the Lower Swansea Valley by the University College of Swansea. It is worth looking at this in some detail, for the project, completed in 1966, was not simply special pleading for a remote corner of Britain. The study concerned itself with a uniquely odious blot of dereliction, but the findings and the recommendations are in great part relevant to the squandered acres of industrial dereliction anywhere in Britain.

Part Two: Ravaged Valley

Chapter 4: The Background

A region, once among the most beautiful in Wales,
was overlaid with factories, pits, spoil-banks, and
workmens' squalid dwellings. Canals came, then the
railways. No one gave a thought to anything but the
speeding up of the industries.
    — EDMUND VALE, writing of the Swansea Valley
    in *Britain and the Beast*

NOWHERE in Derelict Britain is there a more dismaying example of man creating wealth while impoverishing his environment than in the Lower Swansea Valley. A grey-black inverted triangle of 1,200 acres, three miles high and a mile wide base, its apex grazing the very centre of Swansea town, the Lower Valley has been often called in the past the most concentrated and uninterrupted area of industrial dereliction in Britain. This is still true, though some of its scars have been softened in very recent years. And it *feels* true. Because the main railway line from London to Swansea twists for the final three miles like some healthy intestine through the otherwise diseased viscera of the Lower Valley, a visitor's last impression of his journey – and his first impression of Swansea – is shaped powerfully, emotionally by those ravaged acres. And because, moments later and just beyond High Street Station, he comes on a shiny new glass-and-concrete town centre, the shameful valley * of moments before seems by

*I shall use 'valley' to mean the Lower Swansea Valley and, in particular, that part of the valley which was the project area for the Lower Swansea Valley study. In historical references, 'Tawe Valley' or, simply, 'Landore' will sometimes appear as approximate synonyms for the Lower Swansea Valley.

its very contrast the more shameful. In that bright town centre he may well ask how it is that a place so apparently concerned about its appearance, about being a place pleasant to work and to live in (which it is), could at the same time tolerate the most lamentable and repulsive gateway to any town in Britain. The answer is complicated, and so are the industrial activities of centuries which made the valley what it is today. The history of the valley is unique, yet it is also a paradigm of the industrial revolution; similar things were happening in the Black Country, in the North, in all the surging centres of industry which today, like Swansea, suffer the dross of past prosperity.

Green into Grey

Industry – with both its rewards and its penalties – is nothing new to Swansea. Some 250 years ago Daniel Defoe found Swansea

a very considerable town with a very great trade for coals, and culmn, which they export to all the ports of Sommerset, Devon, and Cornwal, and also to Ireland itself; so that one sometimes sees a hundred sail of ships at a time loading coals here; which greately enriches the country and particularly this town of Swanzey, which is really a very thriving place.

Swansea – which without industry might well have become no more than a sleepy seaside town – was already profiting from its strategic position on the sea and on the lower edge of the oval-shaped South Wales coalfield. The coal-bearing hillsides east and west of the River Tawe had been exploited for their riches since the fourteenth century, although by the mid-sixteenth century shipments of coal from Swansea and nearby Neath together totalled no more than 2,400 tons over a ten-year period. By the time Defoe visited the port, population growth and a national shortage of timber had combined with an explosion of industry, and Swansea and Neath were shipping more than 40,000 tons a decade. But even then Defoe found the approaches to the town 'well cover'd with grass, and stock'd with cattle'. Not green for long, not at least the eastern approaches.

For in 1717 John Lane established Swansea's first copper smelting works in Landore in the valley. Other copper entrepreneurs soon followed, enticed by the district's cheap coal for smelting furnaces and the supplies of ore only a short sea journey away in Devon and Cornwall. The Tawe, navigable for two and a half miles from its mouth, was a natural place for industry and Swansea was conveniently located midway between the smelting industry's raw materials and its main market in the industrial Midlands. There was an ample supply of capable labour and an apparent willingness among the townspeople to tolerate the increasingly foul air that arrived with their pay packets.

But the pollution must have been long confined largely to the works themselves and only gradually enveloped the whole valley and wafted over Swansea town. For in 1813 – nearly a century after Lane's pioneer works, and with the valley fast filling up with smoky industry * – David Jenkin was able to write of Swansea: 'The air is very salubrious ... it has induced several invalids to take up their winter residence here and has fully justified their

---

*Margaret Stacey has noted that in 1764 an edict was passed that smelting should not take place within the then (and smaller) borough boundaries. This was one more cause for the concentration of smoky industry in the valley. 'Today's greatly enlarged borough has inherited the consequence of this industrial concentration.'

expectations, by effecting a very beneficial change in their health.' Of that part of the valley nearest the mouth of the Tawe, Jenkin spoke suspiciously briefly, only to praise Sir John Morris's celebrated steam engine – 'the largest in the kingdom' – at Landore Colliery. But beyond Morriston, up the valley, Jenkin found: 'The eye of taste has perpetual gratification from the great variety of scenery that presents itself ... here Nature seems unrivalled in her beauties.' Still, Jenkin was a local boy and, one suspects, unofficially the town's first public relations man.*

By 1823 there were eight other copper works in the valley; together with the collieries and shipping they supported a population of perhaps 10,000 and a circulation of perhaps £3,000 a week in the town. In that year H. Griffith's guide to Swansea boasted: 'Few places in the Kingdom have had so great and rapid an increase of trade as Swansea.' Along the Tawe canal (built in 1798) Griffith counted 'at present carrying on, eight large copper-houses, collieries of binding coal, culm and stone, a copper rolling mill, a brass work, a large tin work, an iron forge, two iron furnaces, an iron foundry, two potteries and a brewery', and he spoke of 'the great extent to which the town and neighbourhood are benefited by them'. Griffith had to acknowledge 'the dismal gloom of the manufactories hanging over the River Tawe' but, a cheerful soul, he found the gloom 'pleasantly contrasted by the whitened walls of their appendant villages'. He was adept at squinting, to see only the long view: 'The town presents a very handsome appearance from the road approaching to it; and in particular, a fine bird's-eye view may be ob-

---

* No doubt Ann Lemmon or, even more, David Thomas – in 1813 the official town crier and scavenger respectively – could have given a more accurate account of what was happening in Swansea. But they probably couldn't write.

tained from Kilvey Hill, whence the whole is brought
into a distinct and beautiful perspective ... charmingly
intersected by the meanders of the River Tawe.' Griffith's
view was probably more to seawards, for he went on to
contend: 'Swansea has for many years become the
fashionable resort of company as a bathing place.' *

Grey into Black

Despite more than a century's growth of noxious industry,
by the mid-1800s, when George Borrow passed there on
his journey through a usually wilder Wales (and found
Swansea town 'a large, bustling, dirty, gloomy place') the
valley was still only grey ('but every object looked aw-
fully grimy') and nature – increasingly isolated in patches
between the prosperous industry – held on: 'I sometimes
passed pleasant groves and hedgerows, sometimes huge
works; in this valley there was a singular mixture of
nature and art, of the voices of birds and the clanking of
chains, of the mists of heaven and the smoke of furnaces.' By the end of the century, nature would have all
but abdicated, the valley black.

By 1850 thirteen copper smelting works had been established in the valley, all sited with the river on one side,
the canal or the new railway on the other. Down the
canals and railways went the coal, up the river came the
ore. Swansea's population had grown from only 6,831 in
1801 to 24,902 in 1851, but the seekers after 'salubrious air'
and the addicts of bathing machines were getting fewer.
By 1854, a more sensitive observer, Charles Frederick
Cliffe, reported: 'The resort of visitors during the season

---

* It seems he was right. The town guide prominently advertised the
fares of bathing machines for the summer season: 15s. for gentlemen,
£1 1s. for ladies.

is not very large, in consequence of the vicinity of the town to the copper works.' He agreed that the industry gave employment to a large number of people – one of the biggest works then employed 500 men and 300 women and boys – who 'appear more healthy than could be imagined, but those not bred to the work from childhood cannot stand the sulphurous atmosphere and heat. The copper smoke is a serious nuisance to the country around, injurious both to cattle and herbage, and has on several occasions afforded employment to the gentlemen of the long robe.'

At night Cliffe found the valley 'no bad representation of the infernal regions, for the smell aids the eye. Large groups of odd chimneys and ricketty flues emit sulphurous arsenical smoke * or pure flame; a dense canopy overhangs the scene for several miles, rendered more horrible by a peculiar lurid glare.' And he found 'the daylight effect not much more cheering, all vegetation is blasted in the valley and adjoining hills, and immense swellings on the joints of horses and cattle occasionally attest the pernicious nature of the vapour. On a clear day, the smoke of Swansea Valley may be seen at a distance of forty or fifty miles, and sometimes appears like a dense thunder cloud.' †

By 1880 Swansea smelted more than two thirds of all

* In 1848 an estimated 92,000 tons of sulphurous acid were emitted into the air by the copper works. The value of sulphur lost this way was estimated at £200,000 a year.

† The Lower Swansea Valley Project report says: 'The continuous envelopment of the valley in fume for nearly a hundred years resulted in almost a complete destruction of its vegetation. The indigenous sessile oak and birch woodland of Kilvey Hill and all grass and heather in the area disappeared. The topsoil, no longer held by plant roots, was washed off the valley sides leaving the subsoil to be eroded into gullies. The area became a virtual desert.'

the copper ore imported into Britain, and other heavy industries in the valley were growing apace. By then there were also five spelter or zinc works and Swansea became as well the nation's principal centre of zinc production. The first tinplate works had appeared in the valley in 1845 and ten more arrived in the following thirty-five years. By 1890 Swansea was the centre of the nation's tinplate trade. At Landore in 1868 the first open-hearth steel works had come; three years later it took a larger site on the east bank of the Tawe and by 1873 was making 1,000 tons of steel a week and was one of the four largest steel works in the world.

'Steel works, copper works, iron and spelter works, tin manufacture – industries that are the pride of those who develop them and the envy of the world,' trumpeted J. C. Manning in 1895. But in fact nearly two centuries of industrial boom conditions were coming to an end in the valley. Copper was declining as the richer veins of ore were worked out and as foreign countries began to export refined copper, and the future of tinplate was unpromising. On 10 January 1891 the *Herald of Wales* announced worriedly that as a result of the McKinley Tariff, increasing the duty in America on imported tinplate by seventy per cent, the first tinplate factory in the United States had opened the previous month: 'Their machinery has been imported from South Wales and is said to be of the best kind, the firm having carefully studied the methods adopted in the tinplate establishments in Wales. Experienced workers have, it is said, been brought from the Principality.' This early brain drain may have been flattering, but it was a sign of the sad and ugly future awaiting the valley in the twentieth century.

Decay

In 1890 only 5,200 tons of manufactured copper had been imported into Britain; by 1900 it was nearly 350,000 tons. By amalgamations after 1900 all the valley's shrinking copper industry came under the control of two firms. In 1921 copper was smelted in the valley for the last time. The zinc industry flourished until 1914, but large-capacity, technologically superior plants developed in America, Canada and Australia during the First World War were able to meet European demand after the war. Between 1924 and 1928 all but one of the valley's zinc works closed, leaving a jumble of deteriorating buildings. Tinplate suffered from the American tariff and the growth of the American tinplate industry, and during the Great War the U S stepped in to meet the needs of Britain's traditional overseas markets. Though Britain recovered her prewar export position by 1925, the first hot-strip mill had started in Kentucky two years before then, a technological breakthrough that Britain did not follow up until fifteen years later (and then not in the valley but at Ebbw Vale and, later, at Port Talbot). One by one the traditional old-fashioned tinplate mills in the valley closed, the last in 1961.

Steel declined similarly; as the tin mills closed, steel-making was transferred to the large Port Talbot plant and to another at Newport. In the valley the blast furnaces of the pioneer open-hearth steel works shut down as early as 1888, and the last steel-making plant closed in 1961. Coal was a similar story. The growth of coal-burning along the Tawe had outstripped the capacity of the pits on the valley floor, and ever deeper shafts had created problems of drainage as well. With improved transport after the coming of the railways in the 1850s, it was econo-

mic to move coal from more distant and more suitable
collieries. Swansea exported nearly 1,800,000 tons of an-
thracite in 1907, but little of it was mined in the valley. By
1931 the collieries had gone.

The valley had never developed what the project report calls 'that richly assorted and adaptable user-
industry that was the strength of the Midlands. Buttons
and buckles, needles and pins were not fashioned in the
arches of Landore.' When the industries that had made
Swansea rich departed, their sites were seldom filled. Zinc-
soured soil, flooded pits, piles of furnace debris, copper-
stained earth, a rubble of decaying buildings were their
final bequests to Swansea.

Desolation

And so in the early decades of this century, as creeping –
and sometimes precipitate – decay rotted away its industrial prosperity, the valley became an increasingly
melancholy landscape. In place of the ugliness made by
men at work – the ever-growing wastes spewed on the
earth, the chimneys spitting foul plumes – came the un-
changing and seemingly permanent ugliness of abandoned work: the cold chimneys dotting the valley floor
like hideous stalagmites, man's dead mountains so foul
that scarcely a weed grew. The ugliness had troubled few
when it was being created: the landlords and entrepreneurs had lived out of sight and smell of it; the towns-
folk had got used to it, the price to be paid for a job every
day. In an age of *laissez-faire* there had been few attempts
to soften the brutalizing effects of industry on the landscape and on the lives of the people who inhabited it. As
industry departed, leaving on the valley floor an estimated seven million tons of dross, there were few attempts

to mend the landscape, to put some green back into the black valley.

One of the few attempts was by George Bell, the apparently too visionary borough surveyor, who in 1912 proposed uses for the tip wastes, the creation of modern industrial sites, a new road and tramway in the valley and 'garden-suburb' housing on one side of the valley. The war necessarily postponed his, or any, redevelopment plans. After the war the dead acres spread over more and more of the valley floor. By the 1920s the canal was semi-derelict and the last barge moved down it in the thirties. No plans to reinvigorate the valley emerged. In those days there was not even an *in*adequate policy for dealing with dereliction and the local authority was not prepared to go it alone.

This is not surprising, to judge from the town's official handbook of 1924, which makes it clear that the local authority was still living in a past of industrial power, that it was unready to recognize either the decay in the valley or the new problem of dereliction. It read more like the muck-and-money tract one might have expected in a town guide of, say, 1865: keen businessmen could find in Swansea 'the desired outlet for their initiative'. The town was

blessed with the horny-handed sons of toil of the right type, men born in the Welsh valleys largely of a Celtic stock who are thrifty and possessed of that grit and courage which displays itself at all times, be it in the factory, the mine, the battlefield or the pulpit. Arduous conditions of labour would appear to have an exhilarating effect upon them.

The guide bemoaned 'the local prejudices which had to be overcome before the industry had full sway'. There was 'no limit to the possibilities of development in the Swansea area'. And in its only reference to the abandoned smelting works in the desolate valley, the guide found it wondrous that 'their decaying walls stand to this day, a link in the chain of industrial effort'.

Widespread unemployment in the early 1930s prompted a government investigation of the nation's depressed areas, and the Special Areas Act 1934 created a fund of £2 million to relieve the social and economic distress of those areas. Though nearly a quarter of Swansea's working population was unemployed, in comparison with South Wales and Monmouthshire as a whole, Swansea was relatively well off and it was excluded from the provisions of the Act. The largest single chunk of derelict land in Wales lay outside the legislation and was not touched. The Second World War postponed further, and more satisfactory, legislation.

At war's end there appeared at last real promise of action to erase the huge smudges of the industrial revolution in the valley. In 1943 Swansea's borough engineer had recommended that the council acquire and clear the derelict sites if central government aid were forthcoming. The Distribution of Industry Act 1945 appeared to be the instrument promising that aid. Swansea became a scheduled development area and for the first time reclamation of derelict land was made an object of grant-aid. But the promise came to nothing. One of the conditions which had to be met under the 1945 Act was that reclamation was necessary for the relief of unemployment in the area. Swansea had just decided to establish a 230-acre light industrial estate at Fforestfach (two miles west of the valley) so the government decided that as the estate would go a long way to cure unemployment, more money to prepare industrial sites in the valley was unjustified.

Besides, the county borough had more immediately

pressing things on its plate: the estate itself to build, industries to entice there, an urgent need to modernize the docks and win back lost trade. On 2 February 1946 the secretary of the Chamber of Commerce said in the *Herald of Wales* that 'Last week not a single general cargo ship was loading or discharging at Swansea docks.' Most of all, some twenty acres of central Swansea had been blitzed by the Germans in February 1941, and an enormous town-centre redevelopment was at the top of the agenda. In the *Herald* of 9 February 1946 a prominent local business-man complained about 'the eighteen months' delay' in starting on the devastated centre. The pressure was on the finances and the energies of Swansea Corporation to deal with first things first. The valley slid back in the queue.

In the 1950s national economic difficulties obliged the government to cut back on capital expenditure, and grants for reclamation of derelict land were severely limited. In 1959 the restrictions were eased and local authorities invited to submit reclamation schemes, but a rigid definition of 'derelict' meant in effect that the land had to be declared of no value to the owner. All the de-spoiled land in the valley was in private hands, and the landowners were hardly prepared to make such a declara-tion. The council was able to level and tidy up only one coal tip which it owned (outside the valley). Between 1945 and 1960 this was the only clearance under the 1945 act in Swansea.

In 1960 the Local Employment Act replaced the 1945 legislation, widening the definition of dereliction, but scrapping the regional development area approach in favour of smaller and frequently altered development districts. These were based on local employment exchange areas in which 'a high rate of unemployment exists or is to be expected ... and is likely to persist'. Swansea's level of unemployment did not qualify it for development district status although the borough's 'real' unemployment was high because of the large proportion of workers employed outside the borough. Prospects for redeeming the valley were again as gloomy as the valley itself. George Orwell's mordant observation of twenty-five years earlier seemed all too true of Swansea: 'In a crowded, dirty little country like ours, one takes defilement almost for granted. Slag-heaps and chimneys seem a more normal, probable landscape than grass and trees.'

In Swansea there was an apathy about the valley smothering all hopes of its redemption. 'The valley was just there,' said one observer. 'A great damn big backyard.' (Worse: it was a front yard.) Only a really energetic initiative would bring decency back to the ravaged valley. As the 1960s arrived, Swansea was waiting – for the man of energy and ideas to provide that initiative.

at this time there was no funding
the money had to be raised.

Chapter 5: The Project

To establish the factors which inhibit the social and
economic use of land in the Lower Swansea Valley and
to suggest ways in which the area should be used in
the future ...
— Terms of reference of the Lower Swansea Valley
Project, 1961–6

IN 1960 Swansea found its man of energy and ideas.
Robin Huws Jones was then director of courses in social
administration at the University College of Swansea. He
journeyed often by rail through those three loathsome
miles on Swansea's doorstep. Anyone who has done the
same will notice that few train travellers look out the windows at the Lower Valley. Perhaps in self-defence – for
the pollution is so intimidating that it seems about to
overwhelm the train itself – sensitive travellers tend to
hide behind newspapers or suck their cigarettes with
closed eyes. The shocking scene is passed in minutes. The
less sensitive may feel, 'What's to look at? A rubbish
dump!' Huws Jones was sensitive *and* he looked. What
he saw disturbed him more on each seeing, and he decided to ask questions: Why had nothing been done?
Could something be done? How could it best be done?

Out of one man's concern grew a remarkable coming-
together of intelligences to find a solution for the valley.
In the autumn of 1960 Huws Jones instigated an informal
meeting of representatives of the University College, central and local government, the press and of the industry
remaining in the valley. They agreed that – apart from
the lack of assistance nationally and the persistence of

apathy locally – ignorance of the valley's peculiar problems and how to tackle them had been a major cause of inaction.

As the *South Wales Evening Post* was to put it: 'The problem of the lost lands of Landore has been complex and baffling. No one has known where to start.' A full-scale study of the valley would not (as studies so often do) merely detail what everyone already knew. A determined and thorough study of the valley – past, present and future – could be a way of breaking out of a static situation. The University College – with its botanists and geographers, sociologists and economists – was the natural machine for the task. John Parry, then the College's principal, saw the opportunity not only to associate the College with the solution of a long-standing local problem, but also to mount a unique inter-disciplinary study within the College. The departments of the College agreed.

An informal working group composed of representatives of the College, Swansea Corporation, the Welsh Office and industry began the difficult job of finding the money – about £50,000 – for the kind of long-term, detailed inquiry required. The Corporation contributed £7,500, the Welsh Office £5,000, and valley industries £1,700; the then Department of Scientific and Industrial Research (now the Science Research Council) granted £11,000 to the College's department of botany for work on the re-vegetation of industrial waste; and the College agreed to provide a contribution in kind – offices, laboratory and technical facilities, and immense chunks of staff time – modestly estimated at £5,000.

This manifest willingness of various interests to focus their enterprise and money on a single problem was a powerful argument for the working group when they sought the aid of a charitable foundation to reach their target budget. Although it was an unusual project for the Nuffield Foundation, its trustees were attracted by the fact that the Foundation would not be the study's only supporters and, as Nuffield's seventeenth annual report was rightly to say: 'The findings may suggest new ways of tackling other stubborn areas of industrial dereliction in Wales and elsewhere.' In 1961 Nuffield contributed £22,500 * towards what was then intended to be a four-year study.

With its financing assured, the informal working group became a committee, and sub-committees were set up. Parry became chairman of the main committee, and a former Colonial Service officer and Swansea man, Kenneth Hilton, was appointed full-time executive director of the project. At a launching conference on 16 August 1961, Parry said there was no intention of making the valley into a 'sylvan glade, but useful and presentable'. The next day the *South Wales Evening Post* headlined: FIRST PRACTICAL STEPS TO RESTORE DEVASTATED ACRES ON SWANSEA'S APPROACH. The Lower Swansea Valley Project had been born.

Area, Organization, Aims

'A blasted heath covered with the debris of Victorian capitalists and litter louts on the grand scale' – this description by Colin Rosser and Christopher Harris sums up the look and feel of the 800 derelict acres which formed the core of the project's study area of 1,174 acres: an inverted rough triangle, its three points touching the village of Llansamlet on the north-east, Morriston on the north-west, and the railway yards of High Street Station

* In 1964 the Foundation added a further grant of £4,150 to extend the appointments of the project's director and conservator.

on the south, the villages of Landore, Manselton, Pen-trechwych and Bon-y-Maen round its sides. An area shredded by inadequate roads and tracks, railway lines, the abandoned canal and the River Tawe, used only for dumping effluents. An area for all its bleakness and decades of decline, by no means dead: in September 1961 there were still no fewer than thirty-seven landowners and seventy-four separate industrial activities in the valley, ranging from a zinc and lead manufacturer employing 821 workers to the inevitable clusters of scrap merchants employing a handful. Although some 8,000 people travelled out of Swansea to work each day, about 2,500 were still employed on the valley floor. 'Economic life is sluggish but not absent,' wrote Huws Jones of the valley, 'suggesting that recovery is not impossible.'

Between 3,000 and 4,000 tons of waste were still being produced in the valley each month, usually but not always disposed of in accordance with conditions laid down by the local planning authority. Excavation of the waste heaps by contractors was not 'development' within the legal meaning of the term and required no planning permission. Conditions imposed on contractors by private landowners were not always enforced and, as the project report was to say, the result was 'a patchwork of excavations scattered throughout the valley with no co-ordination of levels or a planned working programme'. There were also about twenty acres of derelict buildings.

The study looked at not only the valley floor, where the physical problems of redevelopment were paramount, but also at the largely residential valley sides where the social problems were predominant. The survey area had to be considered in the context of the county borough as a whole and as part of an even wider sub-region extending from Port Talbot in the east to Kidwelly in the west.

The project was organized into a dozen separate but co-ordinated studies in two major groupings: the physical problems such as contours, geology, soil mechanics, hydrology and biology; and the socio-economic problems such as employment, housing, recreation, and human ecology. Overlapping both these groupings would be studies of transportation and land use. Research teams set to work on each particular aspect, and altogether six College departments were involved in the project. The administration of the project fell on the director and on the main and sub-committees; the chief executive organ was a steering committee in which the three main interests – College, Welsh Office and Swansea Corporation – were represented. Landowners in the valley, industrialists, schools, the Forestry Commission, volunteer youth groups, and the Regular and Territorial Army were linked with the project.

The overall aim of the project was 'to bring the area back into the natural stream of social and economic use'. This meant first an examination of the obstacles to this end, and an analysis of how to remove them. Throughout the study period, opportunities for immediate practical action would be seized (and were). Long-term action, on completion of the project, was of course the ultimate goal. What the individual research teams found when they started, what they studied and how they went about it, and what they were able to accomplish by way of practical improvements in the valley suggest the thoroughness and professionalism of the five years' work.

Physical Studies

The purpose of the geological survey was 'to describe the surface and sub-surface geology of the project area and of its immediate surroundings, with particular reference to problems of foundation engineering'. The area was first mapped by aerial photographs at a scale of 1 : 5,000, and a comprehensive collection made of all previous sub-surface investigations in the valley. The team sank seven boreholes, four of which reached the rock floor buried beneath the flat, marshy valley, which is about twenty feet above sea level and rimmed by hills of 400 feet or more. Coal seams had been worked to depths of 1,800 feet and the area was pockmarked by flooded pits. The team examined the question of subsidence caused by the collapse of overlying rock into the old workings, and made a comprehensive survey of the existing buildings – some of them built on as much as forty feet of spelter waste – for evidence of settlement due to mining subsidence. A study was also undertaken on the steep sides of the valley where quarrying and opencast mining had oversteepened the sides, 'increasing the tendency of soil creep and, more disastrously, landslip'. Geophysical traverses across the valley floor were made to reveal 'the approximate shape of the north–south buried valley in the solid rock'. The extent and type of drift material found in the area were also recorded.

The amount and complexity of industrial wastes studied by the team were formidable. About half the project area was covered by coal tips, iron and steel slag, factory rubbish, non-ferrous slag, building rubble and current urban tipping. Many tips contained cooled molten slag. Many of these sores on the valley's face contained harmful chemicals. These and the heterogeneous nature of most of the wastes raised obvious problems of the danger to pile-foundations and of settlement of foundations if substantial structures were to be built in a revitalized valley.

The project's botanists, concerned with re-vegetation techniques in the valley, were faced not only with the 800 acres of dereliction – with slags from metallic ores considered highly poisonous to plant life – but another 300 acres of badly eroded, infertile, sandy clays sparsely covered with common bent-grass and wavy hair-grass or spattered with marshes and ponds. Erosion had created the infertile soils after sulphurous smelter smoke had destroyed their original vegetation. The practical objective the team set for itself was 'to develop techniques for the inexpensive establishment of vegetation giving an acceptable cover and requiring minimal maintenance'.

On the most technically difficult metallic wastes, the project chose three experimental planting areas – a steel, a copper, and a zinc tip – and on the more innocuous wastes and eroded soils they undertook tree planting and grass trials. The National Agricultural Advisory Service supplied chemical analyses of the tips and soil, and the on-site trials were supplemented by glasshouse experiments in the College's botanic garden; these involved growing plants from seeds germinated directly in the tip materials and from seedlings transplanted to tip material. Pilot experiments in 1962 with white mustard, common bent and wild white clover were followed the next year by a main experiment with 144 plots, again using mustard and bent grass and also a grass ley mixture that had been devised for reclamation of coal-shale waste in Lancashire. Large-scale seed trials in 1965 examined various fertilizers and pulverized fuel ash as a seed bed.

The project area lies almost entirely within the flood plain of the Tawe, and the hydrology team examined the river's characteristics and their relevance to the project as a whole. Past records told the researchers that flooding occurred on average once a year and that the Tawe was

an erratic, 'flashy' river showing rapid alternation of high
and low flows. Weirs and bridges in or across the river at
points meant that the Tawe overflowed its banks at lower
discharges than if they had not existed. The lower reaches
of the river were affected by tidal influences which could
contribute to the flood problem. Low-lying parts in the
project-area were frequently flooded; these areas were
drained by a small tributary stream, the Nant-y-Fendrod.

The hydrologists analysed ways of solving the flood
problem. They also studied the possibilities of harnessing
the Tawe as a water resource. The river had a long history of pollution by industrial wastes and was still, at the
time of the project, heavily contaminated in its lower
reaches. The team considered the river as a possible
amenity and carried out surveys of pollution and oxygen-
content relevant to the possibilities of introducing fish
life. The team also examined ways to improve the un-
aesthetic appearance of the lower Tawe – caused by tidal
influences bringing polluted water from Swansea Bay
and exposing unsightly mud banks at low tide.

In addition, special studies of the climatology and air
pollution of the valley were put in hand. The climatology
team's work was directed to answering 'whether or not
the valley has any climatic peculiarities which will make
it necessary to limit or modify suggestions for the future
use of the area'. To that end, temperature ranges and
inversions, wind directions and the physical orientation
of the valley were thoroughly examined and evaluated.
The climate – and particularly the temperature inversions of the valley – also had an important bearing on the
air pollution studies. This team analysed sulphur dioxide
and particulate acid concentrations, the effects of
atmospheric pollution on vegetation, and the quantities
of lead and zinc in smoke samples. A physiological survey

of respiratory symptoms and lung function among the valley-side villagers of Llansamlet was also undertaken.

Physical and Socio-economic Studies

Between October 1962 and October 1963 the project's civil engineering team examined the transportation pattern in the valley. Classified traffic routes bordered the valley on three sides, but on the floor itself there were only short, badly surfaced, unconnected works-access roads, and several large tracts of land in the valley were accessible only on foot. In contrast, the criss-cross of railway lines, canals and waterways divided the whole area into a series of small and awkwardly shaped sub-areas. The team was faced with a transport network that hampered the efficiency of existing industries, inhibited prospects for redevelopment and – in the absence of a central cross-river bridge – isolated some residential areas on the valley sides from central Swansea.

The project studied the regional road-movements, to relate the valley's road problem to the larger traffic-flows. The team also carried out a series of roadside interviews and volume-counts on the major roads fringing the valley, and in the light of information on probable land-use developments in the county borough and future population distributions, estimated future demand for transportation in the vicinity of the valley. Studies included the extent and mode of travel to work (by social class and car ownership). The team also examined the existing rail and potential waterways traffic; no waterways in the project area were by then open to navigation. To provide a working basis for the development of a detailed road plan, three outlines of future land use on the valley floor were prepared, ranging from mainly visual rehabilitation to maximum industrial development. The team estimated the costs of road works involved in each of the three land-use proposals.

The physical realities of the valley – its situation in the South-West Wales sub-region, the characteristics of its land, and its inadequate transport network – served as a backcloth for the economic study, which was directed 'primarily towards attempting to determine whether the land was of potential use as an industrial site'. The economists concerned themselves especially with economic growth prospects in Swansea and the region around, and with the suitability of the derelict area to meet any future demand for industrial land. One of the major peculiarities of Swansea which influenced their analysis was the extraordinary size of the county borough: about 24,200 acres with foreshore (21,600 without), nearly three times the size of, say, Oxford or Derby, and by far the largest of any county borough of similar population (170,000) and penny rate product (£28,600). This had meant that – unlike so many large towns in the Midlands – there had never been great land pressures in the borough; there had been no real need to redevelop the valley. Alternative and more attractive industrial sites abounded elsewhere in the borough; at the time of the economic study, twenty-three acres had been laid out with all services at the Fforestfach industrial estate, while a further forty-five acres suitable for development were available there.

In its examination of the South-West Wales background to the valley, the economic team looked at the sub-region's population distribution and movements, migration, and population projections to 1981. The sub-region's labour resources were analysed, as were unemployment figures in the area (3·9 per cent at the time in Neath and the Swansea valley and twice the national

average in the sub-region as a whole) and future employment prospects. In 1963 the team surveyed manufacturing
industry which had set up works in the area since 1945,
including in their sample two industries which, contrary
to the more usual outward movement, had been attracted
to the valley. Information was gathered about the motives
of firms in setting up their establishments, and about
their experience of operating in the sub-region.

The economists then fixed the project area in the context of this sub-region of nearly 500,000 people – and
studied the possibilities of industrial development of the
valley, in line with the project's determination 'to re-
generate the derelict land before it was economically ripe
for development'. The team costed the land acquisition,
earthworks, roads and services that would be required to
reclaim a part of the valley for a modern industrial estate.

Socio-economic Studies

Three studies were undertaken by the project's sociologists – human ecology, housing and open spaces – 'to assess
some of the human factors connected with the dereliction
in the valley'. The sociological survey area included the
villages fringing the valley.* A number of seemingly con-

*The sociologist, Margaret Stacey, described these villages colour-
fully in *New Society* in 1963: 'A typical nineteenth-century street has
a tip at the end epitomizing the close connection of houses and industry. The west side is now almost a continuous urban area,
although the east still appears as a series of villages, connected by
pre-1914 ribbon development. Beautiful at night, when the darkness
mercifully hides the debris, and yellow and white lights twinkle and
float above the chains of orange lights which glow in the valley below,
daytime reveals the confused development. The hillsides are an
extraordinarily patchy mixture of bits of terraces, odd detached
houses, waste ground, tin shops, disused quarries. Many of the roads

flicting and sometimes surprising factors faced the team at the outset, and these influenced its final conclusions and recommendations. It was widely believed that people as well as industry were fleeing from the valley, a view supported by sprouting housing estates on the fashionable west and the north of Swansea; it was said that nobody wanted to live in the valley. Yet between a quarter and a third of the borough's population was still living there, and the valley was not in fact being depopulated. The sociologists studied this apparent contradiction in detail, examining whether it was only the old, the poor and the unenterprising who were living beside the dereliction. The team also analysed the incidence of children taken into care, the provision of free school-meals, and the incidence of juvenile delinquency in order to determine whether the valley was an area with a high proportion of the helpless or troublesome, of families who needed special assistance.

At the time of the team's housing study in 1963, 66 per cent of the dwellings on the valley's sides had been built before 1919, compared to 43 per cent in the rest of Swansea. At the 1961 census 44 per cent of the valley's homes were without exclusive use of piped cold and hot water, water closet and fixed bath, compared with 23 per cent in the rest of the borough. The team was influenced by these

---

are unmetalled and unadopted. The habit of leaving litter about seems to have crept up the valley sides. Unfit houses are left to fall down, garages are stuck oddly on waste patches and tips, their green paint showing up against the grey-black background. Even on new corporation estates, no one cares to remove all the rubble from the unused patches of ground. Above all this, the great stone-built chapels, so typical of all Welsh towns, stand out as a tribute to the strong community life and the enduring faith of the nineteenth-century inhabitants.'

figures in its later housing recommendations, as it was by its analysis of new housing estates in both east and west Swansea and by its examination of the provision of public open space in both halves of the borough.

The team surveyed valley residents about the impact upon them of the visual environment. Two surveys, at six-month intervals, asked a sample: 'Have you heard the ruins and the tips are going to be cleared? Do you think they ever will be? Would you like them cleared?' The sociological study group also related the attitudes they found towards the visual environment to the social and physical isolation of the east side of the valley from the remainder of Swansea.

Practical Action

Academic surveys – particularly when they are devoted to a problem whose solution will involve such customarily unacademic people as demolition workers and muck-shifters – are frequently condemned simply for being 'academic' (in the dictionary sense of 'unpractical ... merely theoretic'). The Lower Swansea Valley Project was determined to avoid this censure and decided from the outset to bring about during the years of its long-range investigations as much practical visual improvement of the valley as its limited finances and manpower and time-for-the-job would permit. This practical work had two unsightly targets in its sights: derelict buildings and un-vegetated ground.

In 1961 the last miles of the main railway approach to Swansea were lined by the abandoned buildings of old copper and zinc smelting works which had closed decades before. 'They had,' said the project report, 'a sad if not savage appearance which was made more striking by their desolate surroundings.' The project did not have the bulldozers and other mechanical plant to sweep them away, but happily Swansea was then the headquarters of a Territorial Army regiment, the 53rd Divisional Engineers. What was an eyesore to the people of Landore or Bon-y-Maen and an adventure playground to the hide-and-seek set of Morriston was to the Terriers a splendid training area for the handling of mechanical plant and for demolition practice.

From February 1962 the regiment set to work on levelling the ruins by bulldozer and winch and demolishing the factory stacks with explosives.* Weekend camps were arranged, and later other engineer units, both Territorial and Regular, came into the valley for training periods. During four years the hideous buildings on five separate sites were removed.† The most spectacular transformation was at the Llansamlet Copper and Arsenic Works: before clearance it was a rubble of collapsed walls and forsaken chimneys; today it is a four-acre grassy oasis pressing impatiently at the frontiers of the remaining dereliction about it. Additionally, British Rail co-operated with the project in removing abandoned railway buildings and signal boxes that had been reduced to relics by energetic vandals, and four sites occupied by obsolete steel and tube works were cleared by their owners.

The tree-planting and grassland trials described earlier

---

*On at least one occasion, enthusiasm unintentionally extended beyond the ruins: an overdose of explosives shattered windows in nearby villages. The Terriers claim that the Regular Army trainees were the over-enthusiastic ones.

†Including one questionable blow-up: the oddly elegant arches of the eighteenth-century White Rock Copper, Lead and Silver Works, which many people feel should have been preserved as a monument.

in this chapter served not only the botanists' aims of determining what plant life in what kinds of surfaces could bring the green back into the once well-wooded valley, but also served, as the project report says, 'as a potential catalyst of opinion and action'. The project appointed a conservator to carry out, with the Forestry Commission, an experimental programme of tree-planting. The landscape architect, Sylvia Crowe, was consulted in the early stages. The project chose mainly the steeper slopes where their planted areas would be less liable to be built over should the future of the valley involve mainly new industry or housing. Schemes for each site were costed and the landowners bore the cost of materials and labour (though the conservator's services were not charged for).

Altogether more than 130,000 trees were planted by the conservator and by the Forestry Commission acting as the project's agent. The project's botanists and the National Agricultural Advisory Service developed and improved the grass on four acres of the eastern slopes of the valley; though primarily experimental, the plots were large enough to be visually effective and served a public-relations end as well. 'There is often an advantage in making large-scale vegetation trials visible to the public,' says the project report.

These new blotches of green soon ran into difficulties that had nothing to do with the poverty or poisons of the soil or the exposed heaps to which they clung. 'The ruins served as castles and dens, the tips as bicycle switchbacks, and the canal was full of sticklebacks,' says the report. 'It was a wild and free land where children could quite literally lose themselves.' Not surprisingly, then, the conservator soon found that the already existing alder, birch and willow had been hacked indiscriminately by undersized axemen, and in the weeks before 5 November much green wood, in a bleak place which could spare none of it, was yearly dragged off to fuel the Guy. 'It was obvious that there was a considerable risk that the new woodlands would be damaged, if not completely destroyed, by the very generation for whom they were planned.' The project considered but rejected fencing and patrolling. The only way was to try to associate the children with what the project was trying to do.*

Since 1962 the conservator has repeatedly visited the four primary and four secondary schools within the project area, shown films and made the children aware of the importance of afforestation and conservation. Four school plots in the valley have been planted and maintained by the children themselves. The conservator has encouraged youth-clubs to look after planted patches – which soon become their possessive 'territory'. Open spaces on the valley floor have been used for school field-studies. Fire is a special hazard, especially in spring when, following agricultural tradition, Welsh farmers burn their rough hillside pastures; the temptation for little boys to emulate is difficult to resist. But the conservator has organized youth patrols who tour the valley to look for fires (and firebugs), put out the small ones themselves and sound the alarm for the bigger ones.

In addition, International Voluntary Service has held summer work camps in the valley in association with the project, students from the Continent joining British ones in stone-picking and digging holes for new trees. And with the co-operation of some landowners, the project erected bollards on some tracks to cut down the large-scale rubbish dumping that a blighted area attracts.

* As Garth Christian wrote: 'To the schoolboy, a fence represents a challenge, something to break through, or to climb over; but trees planted with his own hands are something to care for.'

During the years when most of the project's studies by their very nature could not be *seen* to be done by the people of Swansea, these practical actions to improve the visual environment of the valley were important far beyond the islands of green they established. The grasses that appeared where all was black before, the trees that replaced the derelict chimneys on the valley's silhouette – these were things everyone in Swansea could understand and appreciate. They were not 'academic'. They proved to the doleful that there was still hope for the valley, to the indifferent that they made a difference, to the sceptical that green things could grow there. They were an irrefutable argument for *doing something*. And they strengthened the project's hand on that day in the late May of 1967 when the blueprint for renewing the ravaged valley was presented to the people of Swansea.

Chapter 6: The Blueprint

The vision of the future is of a valley in which people
live and play as well as work, without these activities
intruding much on each other; a valley which offers
the seclusion of wooded slopes and quiet paths as well
as the activity of its workshops; a valley where the
sides and the floor are brought together, not only in
the daily journey to work as in the past, but for shopping and for entertainment, for walks along the river
bank, for games and for school; a valley which, instead of dividing the Borough, unites it in a new
focus of landscape beauty, enjoyment and employment. This is a vision which is quite capable of becoming a reality with the local and regional resources
which are available provided that a determined effort
is made to achieve it.

    – KENNETH HILTON *The Lower Swansea Valley
Project*, 1967

'THE derelict area has been brought into fine focus by
the project' – so did the *South Wales Evening Post* of 23
May 1967 welcome the published report of the Lower
Swansea Valley Project. The project had formally ended
a year before; what had then emerged was the project's
blueprint for redeeming the mangled valley. It was a
329-page, tightly argued manifesto for at last breaking
the vicious circle described by the report: 'The ugliness
of the land has not so far been sufficient to justify its redemption and yet until it is visually redeemed it will remain unwanted.'

    The imaginative blueprint called for a £3 million
revival in the forbidding valley, sweeping away the in-

dustrial detritus of centuries, and replacing it with a careful balance of new industry, housing and green open space. It was more than a blueprint. It was a challenge to the people and the powers of Swansea (as well as to a central government whose assistance would be required) and the local press recognized it as such: 'The problem is vast but the challenge of the report is compelling.'

The challenge was rooted in the conclusions and recommendations of the twelve study-reports * which were integrated into a reasoned overall land-use plan. The machinery to make the plan work was outlined. And – one of the most valuable contributions of all – the blueprint was painstakingly assessed, and its costs and benefits thoroughly detailed. It was this final exercise which distinguishes the report of the Lower Swansea Valley Project from many 'academic' studies, where the visionary is seldom reined by realistic arithmetic. This cost/benefit analysis made it impossible for scoffers to speak convincingly of ivory towers; it made the valley report a hard-headed document whose arguments could be contested but not derisively dismissed.

Conclusions and Recommendations

The study of the geology, soil mechanics and foundation engineering characteristics of the valley concluded that 'the project area is surrounded by and underlain at depth by a series of rocks which generally offer good engineering characteristics, but the project area itself lies almost entirely on a flat marshy plain, consisting in parts of deep deposits of alluvium which have poor foundation properties'. At the same time, the hard industrial wastes,

* A list of the study-reports and their principal authors is included in the Note on Main Sources at the end of this book, p. 227.

the land is fluid alluvium deposits, poor
foundations, but rubble reclaimed some
areas.

The Blueprint

often dumped on the soft alluvium, had in effect 'reclaimed' some areas and were an asset from a foundation
engineering standpoint. The contour mapping had
shown a wide diversity of levels in the valley which would
need to be rationalized in areas to be developed. Although the survey of existing buildings on the valley-floor
had 'failed to reveal any subsidence which can be directly
attributed to mining', notice needed to be taken of two
particular problems created by extensive underground
workings: 'The exact location of old adits, shafts and air
vents prior to [any intended] construction work' and 'the
possibility of subsidence if old flooded workings were to
be pumped dry'. It was also suggested that 'the bearing
capacity of the fill material which varies from one half
to two tons per square foot may, in certain circumstances,
be improved, where required, by the use of vibro-flotation
or vibro-replacement'.

The study of revegetation techniques confirmed that
there were three principal types of derelict ground in the
valley: 'Infertile and largely non-toxic clay loams, badly
eroded by former smelter-smoke pollution; tips of relatively innocuous waste materials, such as coal shale,
foundry sand, furnace slag, domestic refuse; and tips of
waste, poisonous to plant growth and derived from the
smelting mainly of copper and/or zinc ores.' The successful establishment of forest trees and agricultural grass
leys using normal forestry and agricultural methods had,
however, proved possible on the eroded loams and relatively innocuous tips (with appropriate fertilizers). The
revegetation of the copper and, particularly, the zinc
tips would be more difficult, although the incorporation
of lime, a general fertilizer and domestic refuse or sewage
sludge had allowed common bent-grass, an agricultural
grass ley and certain shrubs to become established. But

111

growth of some grasses and shrubs had fallen off after two years and further study was needed to assess their long-term performance.

The botanists recommended that the two non-toxic types of derelict ground could be successfully revegetated for not more than £35 an acre, exclusive of site-clearance and earth-moving. The toxic ground 'should as far as possible be cleared of its tip material by giving priority to hardcore extraction industries'. What remained could be best treated with a six-foot layer of innocuous waste such as town refuse covered by inert material such as spent foundry sand or steel slag; this could be planted after two or three years. This 'reclamation' dumping of domestic refuse might not cost more than normal refuse-disposal; the cost of using sand or slag might be up to £400 an acre, excluding stone-picking, cultivation and fencing. Where it was undesirable or impossible to remove and level the copper and zinc tips, a cover of organic amendment plus lime and fertilizer could be sown to a tolerant strain of grass-seed; this would cost not more than £185 an acre, excluding stone-picking, cultivation and fencing.

The investigation of the River Tawe determined that flooding in the valley was influenced not only by rainfall but by tide, obstructions such as weirs and bridges, and by the filling of flood storage space by tipping. Average flood levels were found to have increased over the previous fifty years. The study concluded that 'The Tawe is only a limited water resource for industry in the absence of any form of water storage' and that 'pollution levels make it generally inimical to fish life, but the position is improving and can be expected to improve in the future'. The quite dramatic recommendations included a levee system to guard the valley against flooding, and a culvert on the Nant-y-Fendrod tributary. The Tawe 'should be regarded in the long term primarily as an amenity', although this was 'not incompatible with its serving industry as a limited water resource for cooling water provided that the water abstracted is recirculated satis-factorily'. The cost of making the river suitable for navigation was considered unjustified and the study recom-mended that the present tidal movement in the river be stabilized eventually by a movable barrage: 'This would transform the appearance of the river and would pro-vide Swansea with a valuable amenity on its eastern side.'

The special analyses of climatology, air pollution and respiratory symptoms in the valley had an important bearing on final land-use plans. The climatology study by J. Oliver found that because of temperature inversions in the project area 'mist, fog and frosts are more numerous and persistent on the valley floor. Shut in by the layer of warmer air above, smoke, fumes and dust cannot easily disperse and are, therefore, concentrated in the shallow pool of dense, cold, stagnant and often humid air.' There was 'evidence to indicate that caution is necessary in using some of the lower parts of the valley-floor', and 'ill-planned layouts of factories or residential areas could easily complicate still further the already complex pattern of air movement and fume dispersal'.

The studies of atmospheric pollution by P. D. Gadgil and of respiratory symptoms by M. McDermott found

no conclusive evidence that the vegetation of the valley suffers from the present level of atmospheric pollution, or that it is a factor in preventing colonization of tip areas. The relation-ship between health and pollution is more difficult to resolve, although the survey of respiratory symptoms in Llansamlet sug-gests that this area at least is relatively more adversely affected by conditions conducive to such chest troubles. Any addition to the present limited sources of atmospheric pollution, whether from new residential areas or industrial processes, either in or on the margins of the valley, must introduce unfavourable modifications in the environment.

Despite the inadequacy of both the existing road network on the valley floor and the peripheral roads around the valley, the highway and transportation study judged that the valley was 'advantageously situated relative to all major elements of the existing transportation network' but that 'this network is fast becoming inadequate to meet the needs of future road traffic'. While conceding that 'there is no significant traffic demand for a new cross-river bridge link in the centre of the valley', the study argued that 'such a link is nevertheless most desirable in terms of the general development of the borough'.

It was satisfied with the port and railway facilities (though a new road pattern on the valley-floor would demand a new railway bridge over a new north–south spine road) but felt that the Swansea canal 'should eventually be filled in when alternative arrangements have been made to meet the needs of industrial water supply'. Also, 'a complete and comprehensive new road network for the valley-floor' and 'a new network of pedestrian footpaths connecting surrounding residential areas with new open space and amenity areas on the valley-floor' were required. There were also recommendations to extend the M4 South Wales Motorway westwards as far as Llanelli, and to widen existing valley-side roads.

The study of the people, their environment and their houses deduced that the population of the valley was 'a normal cross-section of the borough ... except for some shortage of the most wealthy groups' and that the valley was not a problem area breeding unusual numbers of juvenile delinquents or children taken into care. However, this 'normal' population was 'living in a substandard environment', judged by the standards of the borough as a whole: schools and homes were old and in need of replacement and renewal, and there was a shortage of open space per head of population (2.44 acres per 1,000 persons in the east, 7.32 acres in the west) and 'such open space as is provided is of a lower standard than that in Swansea West'. Despite these drawbacks, population was not declining in the valley and in fact new housing was going up – more of it privately built than by the local authority compared to Swansea West. There was a movement from Swansea West to Swansea East 'for persons in the income group up to and just above the national average wage, and particularly of those working in the north, east and south-east of and around the borough'. The attractions of living in the valley area were 'cheap houses and reduced costs of travel'. The study ended its conclusions with a caution: 'The conception of the valley-floor as a problem of industrial dereliction considered separately from the valley-sides thought of principally as residential areas is artificial in terms of the present problem.'

The sociological study urged, subject to more detailed microclimatological investigations, that where parts of the valley-sides needed redeveloping, areas of the valley-floor could be taken over for residential development. Housing, schools and shops, interspersed with open space, could be built on undeveloped land on the east side of the valley up to the railway and on the west side of the valley up to the river, taking care 'to graft new settlements on to existing ones'. Housing could later extend into the central area of the valley itself, if not taken up by industry. Rents should probably not be above £4 weekly (at 1963 prices) and, indeed, there was a case for 'specially low cost dwellings for the lower income groups because proximity to the town centre will reduce their living costs and make labour available in that area'. The study argued that 'the valley should be upgraded and developed to continue to house a quarter of the town's population, including the increases to 1981'.

The recommendations for open space included provision of two parks, one on the east and one on the west of the valley, both running down the hillsides to the Tawe. There should be a riverside walk linking with the west-side park; certain tip areas could be set aside for adventure playgrounds and bicycle tracks; part of the area should be developed as 'free-ranging open space'; playing fields were needed in the northern part of the valley; and the recreational area should include an indoor recreation centre for winter recreation in particular. It was felt that the valley 'should be considered as part of the regional plan for sport and recreation'. In view of these housing and open-space recommendations, 'any severe air pollution in the development of new industry should be avoided' and 'the valley-sides and the valley-floor should be looked upon as one urban-renewal exercise with a master plan'.

The study of the valley's prospects for industrial use, in the context of the South-West Wales sub-region, determined that the total insured population of the whole area was growing very slowly. Metal manufacturing and mining still dominated regional employment and 'the increased substitution of capital for labour in the steel and coal industries is likely to result in considerable future unemployment'. Another thirty to forty thousand jobs would be needed by 1981 in South-West Wales. In the main, new industries that had set up in the sub-region since the Second World War had been successful. 'More effective inducements' were required to attract manufacturing industry and in the absence of an effective policy for industrial growth in the sub-region it was 'unlikely that the comprehensive redevelopment of the valley will be undertaken'. But the study concluded that the valley 'is centrally located in an area of nearly half a million people, and parts of it could provide valuable industrial sites'.

'The visual improvement of derelict land is an essential first step towards its eventual redevelopment for industrial, residential and amenity use,' urged the study of visual renewal of the valley. 'The cost of doing this is low in comparison with the long-term benefits to be obtained, although at present many of these benefits cannot be adequately measured.' The total impression of dereliction and neglect was 'as much an aggregate of a large number of small eyesores ... as a single tip or a derelict building'. The local authority should have powers to deal effectively with such eyesores and the government should consider replacing the Litter Act with more comprehensive legislation.*

'There is some evidence,' said the study, 'that the indiscriminate dumping of industrial rubbish, as opposed to the waste from extractive industry, is the result of uncoordinated policy for its collection and disposal.' A regional study of this situation was needed in South Wales. The co-operation of schools 'in efforts to upgrade the environment' should be continued on a more permanent basis 'and it is suggested that Swansea County Borough Council might consider how this can be achieved'. The participation of voluntary bodies such as the Civic Trust and International Voluntary Service

---

* The Civic Amenities Act 1967, introduced by Duncan Sandys and given the Royal Assent after the project's report, has gone some way towards this.

ought also to be encouraged. The study called for 'an effective dialogue between bodies with statutory powers and responsibilities for planning and development and those voluntary associations of citizens who are actively interested in their civic environment'.

The Land-Use Plan

Swansea's borough development plan dates from 1955 and is based on a survey completed in 1950. On it the whole valley-floor is reserved for dirty or heavy industry. (The Fforestfach estate is marked for light or clean industry.) 'Considerable changes have taken place since then,' said the project report. 'Heavy industry has continued to decline and it is no longer realistic to consider the valley only as an industrial site.' Also, as an industrial location, the valley would have to compete with other nearby sites.* 'Until location policy becomes more selective, not by area as hitherto, but also by industry,' said the report, 'such competition must limit the chances of new industrial use of the derelict land in the valley.' Additionally, with about 2,500 acres of virgin land in the borough suitable for development, and even allowing for possibly lower site development costs in the valley than on hilly land outside it, there was 'no economic pressure to build on derelict land in the valley and no obligation to do so'.

Swansea was a service centre for the sub-region; in 1964 three times as many people had been employed in the

* In South-West Wales at the time of the project's report, there were 2,664 acres of land allocated and/or approved for industry but not developed (including 1,040 in Swansea). Another 3,817 acres were not allocated or approved but considered suitable for industry (including 1,490 in Swansea).

service sector as in manufacturing and it could be assumed that service industry would provide most of the new jobs for the projected population increase of 40,000 by the year 2001. Such new industry as had located itself in the valley since the war had been either of the service type or 'clean' industry such as plastics. The valley could not offer the huge sites required by modern heavy industry, nor could the Tawe meet a heavy demand for industrial water. Finally, the physical state of the valley's land itself – especially the lack of roads and services and the liability to flooding in parts – seriously inhibited its use for industry.

Having argued that the valley should not be completely turned over to industry, the project then put forward its new land-use proposals, with the vital proviso that the valley could not be considered in isolation. 'The renewal of the urban fabric around it' as well as the economic health of South-West Wales and government policies for the area all had important bearing upon the land-use solution.

There were 642 acres on the valley floor available for some future use, and the project considered that 407 acres should eventually be apportioned for industry and commerce, 115 acres for housing, and 120 acres for amenity.*

Despite the drawbacks of the valley as an industrial site there were still 'important advantages' which justified allocating considerable land for industry. The area was close to labour supplies and service industries; it was near a large port, main-line railway and a proposed liner-train terminus; it lay across the main South Wales road from which there were good road links to the M5 and the

---

*Because of the valley's urban situation, agriculture was ruled out: quite apart from the problems of improving the soil, vandalism and trespass would be serious problems.

M4 (when extended into Wales). It was close to oil, petro-chemical and vehicle manufacturing plants; and attractive sea and country for recreation (the Gower) were nearby. 'We conclude that the valley is suitable for both manufacturing and service industry provided that fume-producing industry is avoided. We consider that the sites can be cleared without difficulty and that the area has important locational advantages which merit attention being given to it as part of a regional plan for industrial growth.'

Because of air pollution, industrial tipping and the low-lying nature of the land, few houses had ever been built on the valley-floor. 'But now the situation has changed,' judged the report. 'Tipping has raised the levels and with the reduction in air pollution it is possible to envisage parts of the floor being used for housing in the future if services and amenities are available.' It might however be necessary to designate the housing area as a smokeless zone. Terraced housing on the eastern valley slopes if 'developed with imagination could make a substantial improvement to the appearance of the valley' and could help to 'redress the environmental balance between east and west of Swansea'. Flanking the main railway approach to the town, it 'might provide a "shop window" for imaginative low-cost private or municipal housing using methods of industrialized building'. Costs could be further reduced if housing were integrated with industrial development on the valley-floor.

On the west side of the valley, where much of the housing had been built before 1875, the project recommended a structural survey to identify *areas*, not just individual houses, which were ripe for renewal. It called for area redevelopment aimed at 'an environment in which the surroundings of a house are as important as its interior

1. (ABOVE) 'Moonscape'. Part of a brick-works near Bedford
2. (BELOW) Careless Lane land-reclamation site, Ince-in-Makerfield

3a. (ABOVE LEFT) Littleburn planted pit heap
3b. (BELOW LEFT) Growth of trees on Littleburn waste heap
4a. (ABOVE) Cossall tip as it appeared to passengers on the London-Sheffield railway line when the colliery closed in 1967
4b. (BELOW) The same tip in July 1968 after re-grading work by the Nottinghamshire County Council Planning Department

5*a*. (ABOVE LEFT) Cranford St. John prior to restoration
5*b*. (BELOW LEFT) Cranford St. John restored by Northamptonshire County Council 1954
6. (ABOVE) Mud, stones and rubble in an old quarry in the Lower Swansea Valley area

7. (ABOVE LEFT) Looking across the river in the Lower Swansea
   Valley, with a view of industrial ruins and, in the background,
   the White Rock tip and part of Kilvey Hill
8. (LEFT) A gravel pit at Sevenoaks, where trees have been
   planted to screen operations, *top* 1964, *bottom* 1948
9. (ABOVE) The spoil heap at Brodsworth Colliery

10. (ABOVE) China-clay pit, Cornwall

11. (BELOW) Gilfach Goch

design, in which environment is regarded as the living space of the community as a whole'. Schools on the western side of the valley were old and playing-fields few; the project also proposed a new comprehensive school for the area.

'One of the attractions of the valley, even in its present state, is its remoteness, almost its wildness,' said the land-use report. 'This is a rare quality to have so close to built-up areas and is something we feel ought to be preserved somewhere when other parts of it are developed.' The project proposed that an existing two-acre pond in the centre of the valley be enlarged to ten acres for boating and fishing. A surrounding woodland of over twenty acres had already been planted by the project and was established. A lake and woodland would extend to over fifty acres and form a bridge between the residential areas east and west of the Tawe. The new parkland could be linked to the proposed new housing by a lineal spinney, 'enabling people living east of the river to move across the valley by footpaths through a continuous strip of woodland free of traffic'. A second woodland park was proposed on Kilvey Hill,* rising just outside the project area.

For more than 200 years the River Tawe had provided industry with water and received its effluent, but the Rivers (Prevention of Pollution) Act 1961 had already improved the quality of its water. Sea trout and even salmon had been caught in stretches of the river where ten years before no fish could live. 'As the tips are cleared,' said the report, 'new possibilities are opened up of being able to enjoy the river once more.' As a seaside town, Swansea was fortunate in its facilities for sailing and boating in summer, but in winter there was little sheltered water available. There were, however, problems in

* Progress to this end has since been made. See Chapter 7.

turning the Tawe into an amenity water. Though attractive at high tide, the Tawe at low tide revealed ugly banks of mud littered with debris. How could the river be permanently maintained at high tide – providing a long, wide stretch of safe water for recreation – without causing the river to silt up and increase the risk of flooding in the valley?

The solution proposed was a movable barrage, perhaps a large fabric tube filled with water,* able to be deflated automatically when flood conditions occurred, 'allowing the river to follow almost its existing gradient and in doing so to scour out accumulated silt'. It would cost about £120,000 and 'would transform [a part of] the river ... into a narrow lake 1½ miles long and about 200 feet wide'. The river would be available for small pleasure boats almost all the year and would provide a safe winter anchorage for small craft, which could be brought to their moorings over the deflated envelope. If required a lock could be built at one side of the barrage to allow small craft to come up and down the river at most states of the tide. The river banks would be cleaned up and riverside walks laid down.

A new road system was proposed for the valley, as was a new bridge across the Tawe. The existing canal should be drained and filled once the industrial water usage ended, and much of it could be used as the route for future roads to serve the valley floor. The Nant-y-Fendrod tributary could remain an open channel, at least until a large part of the proposed industrial area was used.

The project also put forward for consideration some alternative proposals, including a reduction of up to 110 acres in the area designed for industry and commerce,

* Such a barrage, under the trade name 'Fabridam', has been developed by the Firestone Tyre and Rubber Company.

increasing the residential area and developing a ten-acre site on the river into a covered games stadium with running track, ice rink and river esplanade. The town's proposed zoo and aquarium could be sited there. 'The whole would form a small version of the South Bank development and would serve the needs of the region.'

For the whole renewal of the valley, the land-use plan proposed a twenty-year target, phased in four stages * and carried out by a single authority owning all the land suitable for redevelopment.

The Machinery

Concerned to avoid piecemeal development of the valley, the project contended that 'there must be a unification of the ownership of the derelict land ... [and] ... the public interest requires at least a share in the ownership'. The project advanced three possibilities for land assembly and the development machinery required: the local authority, or a consortium, or a special development authority.

Since the project area lay within the county borough, where the local authority was also the planning authority, the most straightforward solution would be for the valley-floor and the urban areas requiring renewal on its sides to be designated in the development plan as 'an area of comprehensive development to be acquired, replanned in detail and eventually redeveloped by the County Borough Council'. This procedure had been followed in the redevelopment of Swansea's war-bombed shopping

---

* 'Parts of the valley not scheduled for early development under the land-use plan should be temporarily landscaped to provide a pleasant prospect at least for a number of years. Arrangements should be made to maintain areas already planted.'

centre. The main difficulty was finance. A shopping centre can soon pay for itself; the derelict valley was a much more questionable investment, even allowing for government aid for clearing the dereliction, and standard grants for housing on the valley-sides.

Alternatively, a consortium could be formed of the three major interests in the valley: landowners, local authority and the central government acting through the Welsh Office. All the land would be valued on an appointed day and shares issued to the owners in proportion to the value of their interests. 'The land would then be vested in a single company which could raise development capital and to whom the present income from the land, e.g. from hardcore working or from rents, would pass. The immediate income would facilitate preparatory planning and site clearing.' The local council would participate in the equity by the amount that the rate fund would normally be charged with the cost of roads and sewers; its investment would also include the schools and parks zoned for public use in the borough's development plan. Here too there were difficulties. A private Bill in Parliament would be needed to give the council power to subscribe equity of this kind. The scheme was complicated, a compromise between public and private interests perhaps difficult to arrange. Under such a consortium only the valley-floor could be considered; urban renewal on the hillsides would still be the concern of the local authority, which would then have separate responsibilities for the two areas – an undesirable demarcation.

A third possibility would be a small development authority to take charge of both the floor and sides of the valley – an extension of the New Town corporation idea for dealing with urban renewal and industrial blight. The authority would be financed by the Exchequer, the extra cost of reclaiming derelict land met by grant. The authority should include members of the local council. After completing the purpose for which it was created, in about twenty years, the authority 'would be dissolved and responsibility for the developed area would revert to whatever local government body was then in existence'. Again there were difficulties. It would be 'an authority within an authority' and 'it might be thought ... a sledge-hammer to crack a walnut'.

Of the three proposals, the report concluded: 'In the context of Swansea alone the local authority could probably deal most effectively [with the valley] provided that a reasonable measure of financial help can be provided by the Exchequer, not only to prepare the area for re-use but to carry the council over the lean years when the return on its investment would be small.' But 'if the need for an instrument to tackle urban renewal and industrial blight over large areas in Great Britain is considered, then we think that there is a case for setting up a pilot develop-ment authority in the valley where the basic research has already been completed'.

Whatever machinery was chosen to do the job, the pro-ject stressed the need for a high standard of urban and landscape design, warning that 'otherwise, the area will become a mediocre hotch-potch which will be worse than the present varied and in parts striking landscape'.

Costs and Benefits

The economic assessment (by Professor E. Victor Morgan of the Department of Economics, University College, Swansea) of the land-use proposals was made against the background of the development needs of South-West Wales. The coastal belt of South Wales from Port Talbot to Newport had experienced rapid and vigorous industrial growth over the previous twenty years, but the western end of the strip and the valleys spreading northwards from it had been less fortunate. Unemployment in South-West Wales had been consistently high. The slow growth of the sub-region had been mainly due to the decline in coal mining; a large part of the growth had been in service industries. However, service industries amounted to 'taking in one another's washing' and 'no community can live and grow entirely on this time-honoured process'. The economic assessment urged that 'for this reason further developments in manufacturing are necessary for the economic health' of South-West Wales, particularly in view of redundancies in the coal and steel industries in the sub-region, expected to affect 10,000 men in the following fifteen years. About half the new jobs required in the sub-region by 1981 would be needed in manufacturing, and it was 'against the background of the demand for industrial sites implied in these figures' that the cost-benefit study of the proposals for the valley was made.

The costs and benefits were looked at from the standpoints of both the developer and the community. The basic principles were that 'a developer should count as costs all the net payments that he would have to make as a result of undertaking a project, but which he would not have to make otherwise, and that he should count as benefits the net increase in revenue that he would receive as a result of the project, and which he would not receive otherwise'. A local authority developer, however, should not count costs – which he would have incurred independently of the project – such as for a road which he would have built in any case. Nor should a local authority developer count as benefits the increases in rateable values arising from the project if they were diverted from other parts of the town. The net increase in rateable value in the town as a whole could be counted as a benefit. A developer in the valley 'must count the cost of buying derelict land though ... this is not a cost to the community, and he must deduct from his gross payments any government grants for which he may be eligible, though these do not reduce costs from the point of view of the community'.

From the standpoint of the community, the costs of the project should be compared with the 'capitalized value of the net increase in real national income which it may be expected to yield, and an estimate, made in money terms where possible, of other benefits of a kind not included in the national income accounts'.

The study used the increase in land values brought about by a development as a starting point for a comparison of costs and benefits, but taking into account the fact that 'the development of a particular area of land may have either beneficial or harmful effects on surrounding land, e.g. the introduction of industry creating noxious fumes would depress the value of nearby property, while the creation of a pleasant recreational area on formerly derelict land would enhance the value of nearby property'. The study also considered (though in so small an area it was impossible to measure in £ s d) what economists call 'multiplier' effects: where a development brings new industry, 'the income earned by people in the new industry creates additional spending which provides employment and income for others who would otherwise remain unemployed. There is thus a secondary increase in output in addition to that initially created by the new industry, and the total increase in income is a multiple of the original one.'

The total cost of the development of roads, industrial

and residential sites and amenity areas, as proposed by the Lower Swansea Valley Project, would be about £3 million. The improvements estimated to cost more than £100,000 were: road construction (£835,000), clearing and levelling (£800,000), land purchase (£400,000), a new road bridge (£300,000), sewers (£267,000), the river barrage (£120,000) and flood-control measures (£105,000). The precise total cost to the community would be £2,562,000 (or £2,285,000 without the bridge) and to the local authority developer £2,962,000 (or £2,685,000 without the bridge).

The benefits from the point of view of the community would be 'the value of the redeveloped land for industrial, commercial and residential purposes; the enhanced value of adjacent and nearby land, both within and around the project area; the value of new amenities; and the saving of travelling time and relief of congestion that might result from an improved balance between residential and industrial development in the town as a whole'.

The benefits from the point of view of the local authority would include increases in rateable value created by developments in the valley and 'the indirect effect in making the town as a whole more attractive to new industry and to tourists'. But what outside assistance could Swansea Corporation expect? Cost of land and earth-moving would clearly qualify for government grants for land reclamation in a development area up to eighty-five per cent, though roads and sewers would not qualify. But part of the proposed road programme would rank for sixty per cent highway grant, 'but would have to face stiff competition for a limited amount of money from other road projects all over Wales'. Costs of the proposed housing would probably not be high enough to attract housing subsidies and the small acreage of amenity woodland in the valley would not be eligible for forestry grants. Any expenditure excluded from assistance would attract rate deficiency grant of about ten per cent, though 'in so far as development added to rateable value, it would have the effect of reducing the amount of rate deficiency grant in the future'.

If industrial or commercial buildings were erected on about 100 acres of the valley-floor, they could add over £500,000 to the rateable value of the town – spread over at least fifteen to twenty years. 'Some of this might represent the diversion of development from other parts of the town, but most of it would be a net increase in rateable value.' However, housing in the valley would be almost wholly in place of similar development in other areas and would add indirectly to the rateable value only if it 'released sites in the borough for residential development which might otherwise take place outside it'.

The economic assessment repeated the warnings against piecemeal development of the valley: 'It is essential that the valley should be treated as a single project and developed by a single authority.' The assessment concluded: 'Considering the valley as a whole, on the basis of the present demand for land, it is unlikely that the total value of reclaimed land used for the purposes recommended would cover the full cost of the operation.' However, there would be important indirect benefits to the community as a whole and, with central government grants towards the cost of reclamation, 'in the long term an authority developing the whole area would be likely to get a good return on its investment'.

The blueprint of the Lower Swansea Valley Project – clearly commendable on aesthetic, social and environmental grounds – appeared also to make sense in indirect, long-range economic terms.

Chapter 7: The Prospects

In many ways action over derelict land offers the key
to man's intentions.
   — ROBERT BOOTE, Assistant Director, The Nature
                                        Conservancy

IN the final report of the Lower Swansea Valley Project,
Kenneth Hilton wrote: 'It is natural that we, the project's
committee and its sponsors, who have seen the proposal
develop through the last five years, are concerned that
these pages should not be its epitaph; and that others will
carry forward where we have left off, not only in the
Lower Swansea Valley but wherever derelict land and
poor urban environment are found.' Elsewhere, some
others – if too infrequently – *have* carried forward; and
substantial land reclamation by yet others antedated the
Lower Swansea Valley Project by years.* But what of
Swansea itself? Will this remarkable report generate a
new life for the valley? Or will the report in fact be its
own, if eloquent, epitaph? And here a third possibility
arises: a regeneration of sorts in the valley, but one which
so ignores or contradicts the report's blueprint that it
will be as if five years and the coming together of dozens
of professional minds had never been. Too little may
easily be done; *too much* may also be done, if what is
done is wrong.
   If, as its makers justifiably consider, the valley report is
a useful case-study with lessons for stubborn areas of industrial dereliction elsewhere in Britain, so are the responses to the report a case-study illustrating – with of

───────────
*See following chapter.

course certain exceptions resulting from local peculiarities – how a similar project elsewhere might be received. How has the report fared? What actions have been taken? What hope is there that the project's land-use plan will be realized?

Reactions and Attitudes

As we have seen, Swansea's press reacted with immediate praise for the project's blueprint. This was to be expected, for the editor of the *South Wales Evening Post*, G. Froom Tyler, had energetically supported the project from its earliest days and was in fact a member of the project's main committee. But Tyler – bringing to his appraisal an intimate knowledge of the people and the politics of Swansea – also wisely blended approbation with apprehension. He warned that the project 'must not be allowed to fade. The momentum must be kept up. It may be now or never.' It was a warning as valid today as it was that day in May 1967.

Beneath the tall slabbish clock tower of Swansea's white-stone Guildhall,* county borough officers and councillors have at least publicly acclaimed the project report – and today claim to support its intentions if not all its details as readily as then. In May 1967, Swansea's town clerk, Iorwerth Watkins – who had been one of the two local authority members of the project's main committee – announced the corporation's determination 'to get on with it'. He has repeated this determination since, and says today that Swansea Corporation would 'betray

* On the fashionable west side of the town, far from the eyesores of the valley. Such an achievement when it was built in the depression thirties that it won an architectural award, the Guildhall today has the appearance of a monumental public bath. So rapidly do architectural fashions date.

our trust' if it did nothing or if it allowed the valley to be redeveloped in planless driblets, ignoring the project's call for an overall plan. W. J. Ward, the borough's engineer, says: 'The report made it easy for us to set objectives ... we have confidence in the valley.'

Those councillors who have chosen to react publicly to the project have taken a similar line. The silence of others reflects disinterest or conceals hostility towards the project, its blueprint or, in the case of some of the reactionaries on the council, a long-standing hostility towards the University College itself. Of the 'new guard', Alderman John Allison, leader of the council's Labour majority, praises the report and feels that 'its recommendations could be effectively employed to the advantage of the valley as a whole'. (Meaning the Upper as well as the Lower Swansea Valley.)

Neither of Swansea's M.P.s – N. McBride, Labour, Swansea East; A. Williams, Labour, Swansea West – responded to my invitation for an evaluation of the report and its prospects. Perhaps they did not receive my letters. The local M.P.s were not brought into the project early enough in any case and they have not been sufficiently 'cultivated'. If they were brought in actively even at this stage, it would help.

Central government's on-the-record response can be summed up in the words of a Welsh Office official with special responsibility for land renewal: 'We accept the Lower Swansea Valley Report *in general* [my italics] ... the report has shown us that it is possible to reinstate the valley.'

Reactions among the industrialists on the valley-floor have ranged all the way from outright refusal to state any views whatsoever to accolades for the project's proposals and even active co-operation in the project itself. Yorkshire Imperial Metals, a joint company of Yorkshire Metals and I.C.I., casts and rolls nonferrous metals; it still refines some copper, the valley's only remaining link with its copper history. One of the project's trial plantings took place on the firm's copper slag wastes. The firm owns 114 and leases 15 acres in the valley and employs about 275 men and 30 women.* 'I feel that no useful purpose would be served by our commenting on the Lower Swansea Valley Project,' says the company's secretary, James Atkinson.

George Cohen Sons and Company, a subsidiary of the George Cohen 600 Group, are scrap iron, steel and metal merchants, owning 74 acres in the valley and employing about 50 people. The project trial-planted a disused zinc slag heap and analysed a pond receiving drainage from the heap, both owned by the firm. The Cohen Group's house magazine has published an article praising the project's aims and accomplishments; the article says in part, 'Cohens have been enthusiastic about this operation right from the start.'

Imperial Smelting Corporation (N.S.C.) manufactures zinc, lead and sulphuric acid; its Swansea Vale † works are the valley's last historical connexion with the zinc industry. The firm owns 125 acres in the valley and employs about 760 men and 60 women. Imperial co-operated with the project, helping with grass planting and giving financial assistance. D. A. Morgan, the works manager, describes the project as 'excellent . . . in general we are extremely pleased that this work [demolition, tree planting, etc.] has been done'. Imperial dumps granulated slag and liquid effluents in the valley but, says Morgan, 'We have

* All statistics of land and employees are those published in the project report. There may have been some alterations since then.

† This charming old name for the valley, no doubt appropriate two or three centuries ago, is a ludicrous misnomer today.

for many years recognized our responsibilities to the community and effected major expenditures to improve both atmospheric and liquid effluents.' The firm has recently spent £150,000 on a new clarifier 'to conform to the very stringent standards laid down by the West Wales River Authority to control effluent discharge to rivers in this area'. The firm's waste slag is dumped in a controlled manner and levelled, making up marshy and low-level ground. However, 'there is no question of reclaiming this waste in the future'. Morgan concludes: 'If the recommendations of the project report are acted upon, there will be a very marked improvement in the valley, and we feel that this must be to everyone's advantage, particularly the local inhabitants.'*

And what of the people of Swansea? When the project began in 1961 – as one University College lecturer puts it – 'The town was suspicious as hell ... and some of our professors were not exactly enthusiastic about it.' During the course of the project, in 1963, the University College sociologist Margaret Stacey wrote that the practical improvements the project was making in the appearance of the valley had 'done much to counteract the feeling that "nothing has ever been done and nothing ever will" '. And

* In contrast, two other valley-floor firms did not reply to (or possibly did not receive) my request for observations on the project: the ironfounders and engineers, Richard Thomas & Baldwins (241 acres owned or leased and about 650 employees) and the most appropriately sited demolition contractors and scrap merchants, Birds (Swansea), with twenty-nine acres and about forty workers. All in all, one is forced to the rather dispiriting conclusion that, with certain exceptions, the project has not caught fire with valley industrialists, some of whom no doubt find the whole project a nuisance and who would obviously favour perpetuation of the mess-making status quo, feeling that their tipping freedom would (rightly) be controlled if the project materialized.

it had 'gone a good way to convince people' that the project was 'acting in good faith' and had 'considerably increased the town's willingness to co-operate'.

Now that the project has ended, will this co-operation be sufficiently vehement to see the plan through? Swansea Corporation's industrial handbook says that the project 'has captured the imagination of people in many parts of the country where industry of the last century blighted the landscape'. But has it captured the imagination of the people of Swansea?

Of the townspeople's reactions when the report was published, one academic member of the project says: 'They just didn't notice ... no one was out waving banners.' Of the situation today, he says: 'Swansea isn't boiling.' His summation may be unduly cynical, but there is no doubt that the project's proposals for the valley are up against local attitudes of apathy and of let-them-do-it – and perhaps of lingering suspicions and even outright resistance to renewal of the valley – which are not aiding the prospects.

During the week after the report was published (and splashed on the front pages of the *South Wales Evening Post*) not one reader sent a letter about the project to the editor. One Swansea lecturer attributes much of the local apathy to a combination of the history of the town and the particular character of the people: 'They're cowed by authority ... this part of the world was so long the oyster of entrepreneurs.' At the same time, there was 'a strong sense of kinship in the lower valley, strongly Welsh * ...

* Rosser and Harris determined that 69 per cent of the Tawe Valley residents were culturally Welsh, compared to 46 per cent in the borough as a whole; 84 of Swansea's 142 chapels were in the industrial communities of east Swansea. Margaret Stacey found that 40 per cent of the population of Morriston/Llansamlet spoke Welsh fluently and over half the borough's adherents to the Welsh Free Church

if only we could harness that to the improvement of the environment'. If only – yet at the moment apathy seems to be prevailing, not local patriotism.

Certainly the project has encountered some oblique, uncooperative attitudes. The local press has warned about a general feeling that the project was merely an investigation of what *could* be done, not *should* be done. There has been a widespread attitude that *They* – central government or the Guildhall or the University College – would do it. One Corporation officer agrees: 'A lot of people thought the College was going to do the job ... and that included some councillors.' One suspects that some councillors did not in fact feel up to digesting the formidable project report.

Indeed, this feeling of let-the-others-do-the-job seems to have invaded the Guildhall itself. The corporation's industrial handbook for 1966–7 spoke of the town's 'two faces' (meaning not the ravaged valley and the renewed town centre, rather that Swansea was both 'a leading industrial centre and a holiday area') but admitted: 'Inevitably, industry of past years has left scars, and none more noticeable than those in the once-beautiful Swansea Valley. This "dead land" as it has been called, is now receiving an awakening at the hands of researchers from the University College of Swansea.' The project had formally ended when those words were written; it had been the project's objective to awaken public opinion, the corporation nad central government to the inhibiting problems and the constructive possibilities of the valley. The physical awakening of the valley itself, apart from some de-

---

lived in the valley area. Rosser and Harris summed up the close life of the valley with a quote from an elderly Morriston resident: 'Morriston's a real tin of worms . . . they say "Kick one in Morriston and they all limp".'

monstrations of visual improvement, was not in the project's terms of reference or capabilities. That particular ball was in the Corporation's own court.

These attitudes of waiting-for-others have been reinforced by stronger feelings: a general turning-of-the-back on the valley by many Swansea people and, in some cases, a positive resistance to renewal of the valley. Despite recent house building on the valley sides and statistics showing a movement of average and below-average householders to east Swansea, there is little doubt that a majority of Swansea people would prefer to live in the more pleasing environment of the west – especially if their jobs were within easy access of the west. They would gratefully not need to see the valley ever again. The town clerk comments: 'People are becoming more particular about housing, refusing council houses in the east in hope of getting into the west.' Margaret Stacey, who argues that much of the new council housing in the west is overpriced, feels that many people would prefer to be in the west but settle on the east because of cheaper private housing which they can buy: 'The feeling is "Let's get shot of landlords!"' The observation of an old man * living alone in a small terraced house under the wall of a derelict tinplate works in Landore nicely sums up the sensations of many younger people living in the valley: 'Nowadays they get up on the hills above here and see west Swansea like Moses looking at the Promised Land ... and if they get the chance they're off before you know it.'

It is well established that, at least initially, there was even resistance in some quarters of the Guildhall: the corporation was already a big landowner in the borough, there was no shortage of land for development, and it was

* Quoted by Rosser and Harris.

simply not considered a sensible investment for the local authority to buy the uncommitted land in the valley. Fortunately, this resistance to redeeming the valley has been overridden – at least to the extent that the Corporation has become a landowner in the valley.

In her human ecology survey Margaret Stacey found that eight per cent of the 300 valley residents questioned did not care whether the valley was cleared up and three per cent did not want it cleared. One aged respondent said: 'People stood it in my day, so why can't they stand it now?' Some feared that rates would go up if the valley were redeveloped; some scarcely noticed the immediate industrial detritus, but looked beyond it to the distant hills and spoke of lovely views; some old people construed the question 'Do you want the valley cleared?' to mean simply slum clearance, and at their age they didn't want the upset of moving house. Others felt that if the ruins were to be cleared only to bring in more noisy, dirty, smelly industry (and this appears now a distinct possibility) they 'would rather keep the ruins, thank you' – at least it was open space, quiet if ugly. Yet others were fearful that clearing up the valley might mean less employment; it could 'do the men out of a job'. This response was met especially among older women born or brought up in the hard years between the wars; their fears and superstitions about unemployment contributed to their resistance to reclamation of the valley.

Criticisms and Evaluations

The report of the Lower Swansea Valley Project was widely and rightly praised in the press, national as well as local. But this does not mean that its conclusions and recommendations are immune to criticism, nor that the valley must be renewed in precise conformity with the project's land-use plan. Indeed, the report itself was clear on this point: 'While the plan presented is designed to meet the needs of the area in an economical way it should be emphasized that these needs could undoubtedly be provided by alternative plans.'

General criticisms both of the structure and functioning of the project and of the validity of its proposals have been raised – in some cases, it should be noted, by the project's participants themselves. Much has been made of the inter-disciplinary nature of the project, the integration on a single objective of six departments of the College, supplemented by outside co-operation from Swansea Corporation, industry and central government. In fact, the feeling of some academic members of the project is that it was more a *multi-* than an *inter-*disciplinary exercise, each of the departments working more or less in isolation, and that the integration of their separate studies into a coherent whole was due mainly to the skilful conciliation and editing of the project's director. But this is not a criticism worth lingering over: whether multi- or inter-disciplinary, it was an extraordinary accomplishment: if it did not bash down academic compartments, it at least blurred the rigid lines and got a variety of disciplines (and personalities) to work together for a common objective. Anyone familiar with the proud and sometimes jealous academic empires will appreciate the accomplishment – and at least in the area of land reclamation it has been accomplished on such a scale nowhere else in Britain.

An allied criticism is that some heads of departments or senior lecturers – either because of a lack of commitment to the aims of the project or because of the burden on their time and energies represented by the project –

turned over the task to junior staff. It is possible that to a limited though understandable extent this may have happened: it is understandable because senior academics generally have more work than they can cope with. To expect them to take on such a major and time-consuming burden as the Lower Swansea Valley Project turned out to be may be too much to ask.

A more thoughtful criticism, which bears on both the composition of the project and the cogency of its report, is that no professional planner was brought in from outside to evaluate the findings and, from a position of detachment, draw up the final land-use plan. As one member of the project puts it: 'The same people who made the separate reports had to put their heads together to make proposals ... and we were all amateurs.' This is over-modest: within their academic fields, the participants were very much professionals, and the quality of their reports is confirmation. It is however true that none were professional *planners*. Yet, on a budget of £50,000, it would have been financially impossible for the project to bring in a consultant planner at an early stage, or perhaps even at the very end of the research. And it is questionable whether a professional planner in any case, having been denied all participation in the fact-gathering, would have agreed to make land-use proposals at a later stage. (The Swansea borough engineer, who is also a planner, and his planning assistant were co-opted members of the project's land-use committee, and planners and landscape architects from other universities visited Swansea and discussed the problems of the lower valley, so the project was not without professional expertise.

The proposals of the report have been called too tame, too much a compromise, some first drafts blue-pencilled practically out of existence. Whatever truth there is in these suggestions, it is not surprising nor entirely a damning deficiency. Any serious study which involves a wide range of people and interests, and particularly if it impinges on politics to the extent that the Swansea project did, is bound to end in consensus and compromise and even some degree of appeasement.* In part this is regrettable, but in part it is only a sensible recognition of conflicting interests and a reflection of the project's realism. The prospects of the project's proposals being realized would be bleaker than they are had the report chosen to offend some of its own participants, the local authority, the Welsh Office and industry.

For example, there is no doubt that some of the project's members consider the industry/housing/open space ratios very much a compromise and are unhappy that the land-use plan visualizes twice as much industry as housing and open space put together; they should have liked to see the proportions reversed.† But open space does not pay for itself in *measurable* terms; industry does. With £3 million involved, an 'uneconomic' return on most of a renewed valley would not have been palatable in the Guildhall in Swansea or the Welsh Office in Cardiff. Nor would many valley-floor industrialists have been receptive to a plan for considerably more housing near their works; their continuing pollution of the land and air would in that event be more severely questioned and their sometimes indiscriminate dumping of wastes curtailed – inconveniently for them. Thus the project report must be seen as a *realistic* document; if it appears too uncritical of

* As pointed out earlier, appeasement (commonly of industry) to the point of self-emasculation has been a characteristic of most reports on industrial dereliction.

† I agree, and there are many statements and hints in the report itself that suggest many of the participants did not visualize the 400-odd acres of industry that emerged on the land-use plan.

the local authority's inaction, of the lack of firm direction and assistance from central government, of those valley industries which were uncooperative, there are obvious reasons. In any event a careful reading of the report reveals more censures than censors – though they must be extracted from the dexterous phraseology, and they sometimes exist only between the lines.

The most informed and constructive evaluation of the substance of the project's proposals has been made * by a former deputy town clerk of Swansea, D. F. Banwell, now general manager of Runcorn Development Corporation. Banwell judged the report 'worthy of serious study by any town planner or, indeed, anybody who is concerned with urban renewal, industrial development, or the treating of areas of dereliction' and he considered ('taken overall') the proposals to be 'particularly well thought out ... if they were implemented just as they stand they would represent an immense improvement upon existing conditions'. But he was unhappy with the project's terms of reference – 'which must have had a most inhibiting influence' – meaning that the valley had not been examined in the context of the development of the county borough as a whole. This, felt Banwell, had resulted in the plan's 'disappointing' and 'inadequate' suggestions for a road pattern: 'a product of the nineteenth rather than the twentieth century'. He urged that the highway authorities examine 'the road pattern not only for the project area but for the town as a whole before committing themselves to expenditure'.

Alderman Allison believes that the project report 'has not laid enough emphasis on the need for keeping industry and housing/amenities at a reasonable distance. If

---

* First in *Town and Country Planning* in November 1967, and amplified more recently in correspondence with me.

possible, a woodlands and park should be sandwiched between the two. And separation is not enough: residential areas should not be adjacent to the roads servicing industries, since, apart from the inherent danger, noise is a nuisance to be discouraged'.

Dangers and Difficulties

In a rather wistful footnote to the published project report, it is suggested that the valley might be revived by 'a T V A * in miniature perhaps'. It is apparent that nothing so dramatic as this is going to happen in Swansea, that on the contrary some formidable dangers and difficulties stand between the proposals and even a modest result. Perhaps the greatest danger is simply that the project has ended and the momentum which it created over five years is running down, and could vanish entirely. Also, many of the principals most involved in the project are no longer in Swansea to keep up the impetus.†

---

* Tennessee Valley Authority, the great American federal corporation created by Congress in 1933, its purpose being, among other things, to harness the Tennessee River for navigation, flood control, and production of electric power for the 4.5 million people who live in its valley. In pursuit of its objective, the T V A has reclaimed large areas of wastelands.

† John Parry, the project's chairman, has taken up an appointment at Yale University; Kenneth Hilton, the director, is now secretary of the University College of South Wales and Monmouthshire, Cardiff; Robin Huws Jones, the instigator of the project, is now the principal of the National Institute for Social Work Training, London; F. Blaise Gillie, the Welsh Office's member of the project committee, left Swansea before the project ended. Sadly the project's vice-chairman, R. B. Southall, died in 1965, and the more recent death of Alderman Percy Morris, who was chairman of the parliamentary committee of Swansea council and a member of the project's main committee, has deprived the project of a powerful and zealous on-the-spot advocate for renewing the valley.

Today, along the railways, the roads and tracks on the valley-floor, miscellaneous rubbish is again being contemptuously strewn. Most of it – worn-out mattresses, building rubble, bits and pieces of hardware – is small stuff and could be cleared by a platoon of husky volunteers in a weekend.* But it isn't being cleared, and if one raises the questions with officers at the Guildhall the response is shrugs and indulgent smiles: it is human nature to dump junk and where more natural a place than the valley? The project report anticipated this situation, warning that its measures to reduce uncontrolled industrial tipping and domestic rubbish-littering would 'deteriorate quickly with the termination of the project unless steps are taken to prevent it'. Steps have clearly not been taken.

Fortunately there is little evidence that the contempt for the valley has extended to vandalism of the trees planted by the project. The signs announcing YOUNG TREES – TAKE CARE are still there, if peeling, and though the islands of green may be ringed by contractors tearing the tips into grotesque shapes or by rusting abandoned cars (on average three a week are dumped on the valley-floor) most of the trees are still there – the project's best advertisement and reminder. The project also anticipated the danger to their plantings that could result from vandalism, fires (which would seriously undermine the report's proposals for wooden open space) or simply no after-management when the project ended. A conservator with special responsibility for the conservation of planted areas would be maintained until September 1968; happily this has now been extended to late 1969, the conservator's salary in both 1968 and 1969 paid by Swan-

---

* The kind of thing I V S has done and could do again. But due to a withdrawal of premises, the future of I V S summer camps in the valley is now in doubt.

sea Corporation. His appointment ought to be continued indefinitely.

The project report recommended that 'a special advisory group be constituted not only to maintain the existing tree-plantations and grassed areas but also to provide continued technical information and advice to whatever authority is ultimately charged with revegetation under the land-use plan'. Although a senior lecturer in botany at the College, Gordon Goodman, received a generous grant of £4,280 from the Natural Environment Research Council to continue studies of waste-tip reclamation for another two years after the end of the project and in 1968 another grant of £2,000 for an additional year, there has been no progress so far to establish the suggested advisory group. Also, at the time the report was published, and at intervals since, the *South Wales Evening Post* called for a local committee to back the project's proposals. Such a ginger group has yet to appear. In the absence of a really enthusiastic, publicly spirited civic group, the impetus of the project is the more likely to fade.*

Finance is a major difficulty, even if an 85 per cent reclamation grant and as much as 10 per cent rate deficiency grant are forthcoming. Even 5 per cent of £3 million – £150,000 – is a lot of money for an authority with a below-average rateable value. Yet Iorwerth Watkins considers that even 15 per cent of the total is 'not beyond our resources ... we must be capable of paying it'. But the argument does not (or should not) hinge on whether or not the total cost is large (it is) or Swansea's share large (it is) but on how to raise and use the money. This has

---

* Probably one reason why a strong civic group has not appeared in Swansea is that such groups are almost always middle-class and predominantly Conservative. The local Labour council is hardly sympathetic to being told what to do by such a group.

not been settled by Swansea Corporation and the Welsh Office because the future of the valley has not yet been settled. But some months ago the Welsh Office did give the borough loan consent to acquire a further 278 acres in the valley at a cost of £80,000, and there is hope in a Welsh Office spokesman's comment that 'the squeeze hasn't squeezed Wales so much ... it is initiative more than finances which is hampering us'.*

But as Watkins asks, 'Where does the valley come on our list of priorities?' That – and what is to be done with the valley – must be answered before the difficulties of finance mean anything. Robert Arvill, in *Man and Environment*, argued that 'a financial "weighting" of the long-term value of the rural areas around Swansea for agriculture, amenity, recreation and so on, would probably reveal that it would be cheaper to develop the waste lands in the urban area than to take more of the (apparently cheaper) countryside'. Arvill did not spell out the type of development, but presumably meant industry and perhaps housing. D. F. Banwell, who feels regrettably that the valley will be re-industrialized, says:

The whole difficulty of the rehabilitation of the valley arises from the financial problems which it creates. The local authority must endeavour to obtain the highest yield, in money terms, from any land which it rehabilitates. Under present circumstances the only way that they can do this is to make sure that the land is used for industry or commercial purposes; redevelopment for residential or amenity purposes can offer no similar incentive in terms of rate income or income from property. The local authority is therefore faced with a situation in which there is no real choice.

Another difficulty is whether Swansea Corporation has

* He was speaking of reclamation of derelict land in Wales generally, not of the Swansea Valley specifically.

sufficient resources of manpower and expertise to under-
take the actual renewal.* As Margaret Stacey has pointed
out: 'The chief planning officer is also the borough engineer and his planning staff is inadequate to do more
than carry out their statutory function of development
control.' However, Watkins says that the corporation
would be quite prepared to bring in outside consultants
if required. The Welsh Office's derelict-land unit could
offer some assistance. Even so, the valley – as one University College lecturer puts it – 'is a classic case for region-
alism'. But of course there is no strong regional body or
machinery in existence, and because of the present local
government structure even Glamorgan County Council
has been unable to play any part in the project or its
future; many observers in Swansea regret that. The
Welsh Office ought to be able to require Swansea to produce a new development plan for the valley; it can't, and
its control and influence over the county borough are
limited.

The proposed reshaping of local government in Wales,
although it should speed reclamation in other parts of the
Principality, promises little for the valley. It is proposed
that Swansea remain a county borough, as recommended
by the 1961 report of the Local Government Commission,
and 'continue to have the functions both of county and of
district council'. If the re-organization as proposed goes
through – and it is far from assured that it will – Swansea
may end up with *wider* rather than narrower discre-
tionary powers. Whether those powers will be used to

* This was obviously very much on the minds of the project's committee members, though they were not so indiscreet as to say so
in the published report. But their casting-about for alternative
machinery – a consortium or a special development authority – sug-
gests that they were not convinced of the local authority's capabilities.

push ahead with the proper revival of the valley is questionable. John Allison, who would like to see both the Upper and Lower Swansea Valley rejuvenated together, says:

The area that lent itself so profitably to the industrial revolution should now be planned carefully by *one authority*. It is most regrettable that this was not recognized in the recent proposals for the re-organization of local government in Wales. It is claimed by the Welsh Office that changes in local government must be evolutionary. But time is not on our side.

Actions and Inactions

'Time is on our side,' claims Swansea's engineer, W. J. Ward, of the valley's future. 'And no time has been lost.' Certainly things are happening in Swansea – though few of them in the valley. A land registry office for Wales has come to Swansea, a motor-licensing centre is coming, British Transport Docks Board is building a £500,000 roll-on/roll-off ferry terminal at Swansea port. None of these developments is in the valley, but some observers consider that the motor-licensing centre could logically have been steered to the valley; a white-collar office there would have been a great stimulus to a facelift of the derelict acres. The Board of Trade is negotiating for thirty-five acres of land near Landore for an industrial estate. The Board of Trade's decision may well have been prompted by the proposals of the project. However, one of the subjects which the project did not consider was the effects on the valley of possible Board of Trade policies. The new industrial estate may conflict with, rather than complement, the project's proposals. The Board of Trade obviously wishes to acquire a site that will involve it in a minimum of land reclamation and which is near to existing roads; the corporation obviously wants the Board to accept a more difficult site. And near Morriston, just north of the project area, a factory to manufacture carbon brushes and crucibles is to be built on a forty-acre site.

This development has resulted in the corporation fulfilling one of the recommendations of the project: the landscaping of the White Rock tips on Kilvey Hill. The old ruins of the White Rock Copper, Silver and Lead Works, at the foot of the hill, had been demolished by the Army between 1963 and 1965. The White Rock slag heap had been attacked for fifty years for road making, leaving hideous ridges and depressions. In September 1967 the corporation acquired the freehold to thirty acres, including the tip area and Kilvey Hill. Part of the hill has now been contoured and grassed as an amenity area, and 350,000 tons of copper waste have been removed and used to raise the site for the carbon-brush factory farther up the valley. A Welsh Office grant underwrote the scheme, which cost £220,000 for land acquisition, earth-moving and rehabilitation of the derelict land for the new factory.

Swansea's past history of inaction over the valley does not promise great things for the future. Iorwerth Watkins recalls council meetings of the 1920s and '30s when it was repeatedly said that 'something must be done about Landore'. But it wasn't. Some of the causes have been discussed earlier. D. F. Banwell adds:

It appears to me that the reason why redevelopment did not take place sooner was that nearly all the factors in the situation discouraged any development, whether private or public. Parts of the area are subject to flooding; the area is honeycombed with old mine and canal workings; the road pattern is not only inadequate but the physical conditions are such that connection to existing roads is inevitably expensive except along the northern edge. Therefore one had the worst possible combination of circumstances: it was expensive to get into the site and, having got into it, the ground conditions were such that building was likely to be expensive. When one also adds factors such as the lack of vegetation, and the sociological problems associated with the area there is little wonder that the Lower Swansea Valley Project was necessary before any progress could be made.

However, under the stimulus of the project, one very promising and very important thing *has* happened: during the course of the project, and since, the corporation has acquired or is now negotiating for about 600 acres in the valley – nearly all the uncommitted derelict land in the project area. Ward says that the corporation is prepared to use compulsory purchase orders for remaining acquisitions if need be. This means that the project's key recommendation – that *one* authority assemble and develop all the land – is well on the way to fulfilment. Ward claims, 'We've overtaken the project report ... something is being done and will be done in the valley.'

Apart from the assembly of land under one authority, it is discouraging that there are as yet few signs of co-ordinated activity in the valley. There are still scrap merchants mucking up the valley-floor, two of which a borough officer admits are 'messy'. Ward contends that 'the itinerant scrap merchants will go early on ... and we will require [tree] screening for the solid scrap merchants'. But a member of the corporation's estate agent's office says that the scrap dealers 'perform a useful function ... they've got to go somewhere'. The plundering of hard-core in the tips has yet to be planned so that it becomes constructive and serves also the end of redeeming the valley. Margaret Stacey has written: 'The winning of hardcore ... could help with the final redevelopment of the valley within such a plan rather than all the time making this more difficult by working at random to a multiplicity of levels, leaving minor mountains in one area and caverns in another.' Much as the contractors go round the difficult solidified boulders of slag, so is there a danger that the whole redevelopment of the valley could proceed in the same way: doing the easy bits first, postponing the stubborn.

It is encouraging, however, that the Welsh Office, Board of Trade and Swansea Corporation have set up a working party to prepare a 'master plan' for the valley. The Welsh Office requested that it initiate the working party, and the local authority agreed. The Welsh Office considers that the new Town and Country Planning legislation, which provides for 'action area maps', should fit the valley situation perfectly.* But so far no master plan has emerged and anyone who suggests that it is past time for an unequivocal statement of what parts of the project's blueprint the authorities agree with and what precisely they are going to do about the valley is considered unduly impatient. It is pointed out that the project itself spent five years on its plan; how could the authorities be expected to produce their master plan so soon? They choose to ignore the fact that they have a completed land-use plan for consideration before them, that most of the essential research has been done for them. Until the master plan arrives, the 'unduly impatient' must be satisfied

---

* The 1968 Act also ends the previous ruling that after four years unauthorized development becomes established and is immune from enforcement of planning control; the local authority will be empowered to serve a notice requiring the immediate stoppage of any operations which are the subject of an enforcement notice. At least one of the valley's scrap merchants – which established 'user rights' after four years – could be evicted under the new legislation.

with the tentative promises of Swansea's industrial handbook: 'Grass and trees are now springing up where for years nothing could grow. Gaunt, ugly ruins have been razed and levelled, and *it may not be long* [my italics] before the area is completely restored.' But 'restored' in what manner, to what ends? And how long?

What Land-Use Plan?

For reasons already suggested, the project's land-use plan calls for a disproportionate amount of industry. Yet redundancies, current and threatened, in the coal and steel industries are undeniably a powerful argument for re-industrializing the valley, as are the pressures for a money-yield that only industry could provide. It is apparent that Swansea Corporation is thinking primarily in terms of industry.* Yet the facts remain that about a quarter of Swansea's Fforestfach industrial estate is still unoccupied, more than two decades after the estate was established; that industrial sites are begging at Cwmbran New Town fifty miles away; that some industries in the valley report great difficulties in attracting top staff to their ugly surroundings. In particular the wives of prospective staff have the erroneous impression that Swansea is an unattractive place to live. It isn't: quite the contrary. But the advertisement of the valley gives that impression. Will light, clean industry come to the valley? It is unlikely, unless the derelict land is first given a complete facelift and generous chunks of land are reserved for green space. Will heavy, dirty industries come? They might – although as W. J. Ward admits, 'The worst thing about the valley is that it's a valley,' and really large sites

---

*The Corporation is also negotiating for another 1,000 acres for industrial development just north of the Lower Valley.

simply can't be created. If dirty industry does come, bringing noise and pollution with it, Swansea in the year 2000 could easily end up with yet another 'Landore' on its hands.* This does not appear to trouble at least one senior member of the borough engineer's staff, who subscribes to a rather alarming theory of 'industrial growth/prosperity/decline/dereliction', a cycle which he considers inevitable. But D. F. Banwell's critique of the project report summed up the dangers of allowing re-industrialization to dominate the land-use plan: 'For over a century the valley has, in one sense or another, been poisoning the heart of Swansea; surely this shouldn't be perpetuated.'

W. J. Ward predicts that in the valley master-plan, 'an area will be earmarked for housing'. So far there is no public evidence pointing this way. Housing, of course, is a complicated issue which cannot be extricated from local politics. The Parliamentary constituency of Swansea East is a safe Labour seat (or was until the by-election evidence of 1967 and 1968 began accumulating) but Swansea West is marginal. The fact that the corporation has built more council housing in the west than in the east is seen by many local observers as a bit of electoral 'packing' – filling up the west with Labour supporters. There has also been an understandable feeling among local socialists of 'Don't put our lads in the valley' and 'Why should the better land and better amenities of the west be reserved for the middle class?' Unless the valley is aesthetically rejuvenated, these emotions are likely to persist and

---

*The project report worried about this, noting that 'in the minds of local people the valley's industrial history has made it a "natural" location for modern industry. This ignores the fact that the locational advantages which were once suitable for heavy industry do not apply today.'

discourage new housing in the valley. Which means, again, generous stretches of green open space, making the valley a pleasant place to live in.

But no one at the Guildhall or Welsh Office speaks of that 'unprofitable' open space. The Duke of Edinburgh did in his preface to the published project report: 'The legacy of the exploiters and polluters will be erased by new trees and houses and grassy slopes. The green will be back in the valley.' His optimism – over-optimism, it may prove to have been – was supported by the report:

The valley has been an industrial site and rubbish dump for so long that it is difficult to imagine it as anything else. Yet it is still a river valley, and underneath the skin of its desolation there are the bones of which scenic beauty is made – sweeps and curves, high bluffs and the twisting river ... its ugliness is really only skin deep and the image of 'Landore' can be changed into 'something rich and strange'.

Banwell says: 'The valley, with the River Tawe, could, with suitable grant aid, have been transformed into one of the most delightful residential and amenity areas of the town, with the industrial areas kept at the back of the town.' *Could have been* – he considers the re-industrialization unavoidable; it is already too late for dreams of a green valley.

Yet a visitor to the valley, seeing its nature-made beauty spoiled by man, can half-close his eyes and see the valley's potentialities appear; certainly, he may well conclude, why not simply sweep away the detritus of centuries of industry, do the minimum of earth-moving required, and turn the now loathsome great triangle into a great rough parkland, a green welcome to Swansea, a lung for the people of east Swansea? Here, under the new Countryside Act, there is a wonderful opportunity for the Forestry

Commission and local authority to get together on providing a 'town forest'. Here Abercrombie's 'green wedge' concept could really take root. As the Civic Trust has put it: 'Many of our great towns have areas of derelict or unused land within or near their boundaries. These could be linked with existing open spaces to form leafy corridors from the centre to the edge of the town.'

'Uneconomic', the leafy corridors? Perhaps, but surely in Britain – an 'advanced' and relatively rich nation – we can afford to make our towns and cities habitable. Surely we can afford to redeem the mistakes of the past when the opportunities arise – and the ravaged Swansea valley is such an opportunity. The project has already put some green back into the valley. Will those patches be a sufficient argument for more – or even a sufficient argument for their own survival? 'Trees are emotional,' says Kenneth Hilton, 'once they are there people are unlikely to rip them up.' Iorwerth Watkins agrees: 'Where there are trees, we are bound to think twice.' But if the future pattern of the valley does not only preserve the green that is there but adds to it generously – more generously than the project report proposed – the people living on the hillsides of the valley will continue to live in a scene not all that unlike the Aberfan one which Dennis Potter described in *New Society*: 'Generations of filth thrust at them as soon as they opened their doors, decades of dirt and more dirt pressing in like an avalanche upon ... the houses of a stinking valley.'

The Lower Swansea Valley deserves something better than this. The Lower Swansea Valley Project deserves action – but action of the right kind. It will cost money, but what is it costing Swansea to leave the valley derelict? The project advanced a solution to dereliction in *human* terms; any human actions that follow must bear that in mind. Until the valley is revived in the right way, in human and not simply economic terms, Prince Philip's reproof holds true: 'The Lower Swansea Valley today is a stark monument to a thoughtless and ruthless exploitation, and while it remains in its present state it is a standing reproach to each generation which shrugs its shoulders and looks the other way.'

Part Three: Redeemed Lands

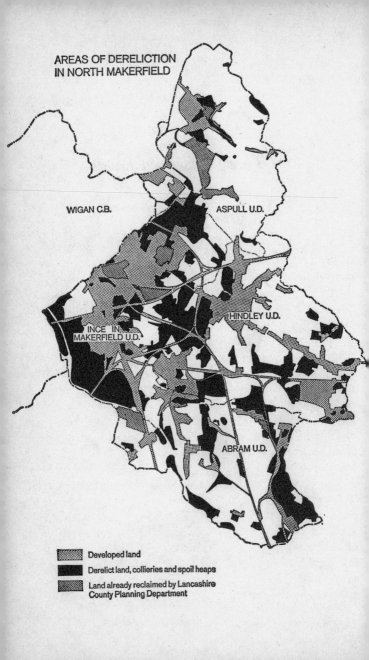

AREAS OF DERELICTION
IN NORTH MAKERFIELD

WIGAN C.B.

ASPULL U.D.

HINDLEY U.D.

INCE IN
MAKERFIELD U.D.

ABRAM U.D.

Developed land

Derelict land, collieries and spoil heaps

Land already reclaimed by Lancashire
County Planning Department

Chapter 8: The Successes

> ... our generation, sicken'd by the grime
> of murky slums, slag-heaps and sooty bushes,
> wil plan garden-cities and for her soilure
> make reddition to Nature ...
>
> —ROBERT BRIDGES *The Testament of*
> *Beauty*, 1929

IN that it has charted out a route to sensible land redemption, its signposts explicit, the Lower Swansea Valley
Project is already a success. But so – in the opinions of
many – were the proposals, say, for Hook New Town or
those for a new growth centre in mid-Wales, the one long
vanished into the dustbin, the other a seeming candidate
for similar treatment at the next great spring clean of
plans-never-to-be. Apart from serving as a model (and a
goad) for similar studies elsewhere, apart from represent-
ing an admirable coming-together of intelligences to remove a monumental eyesore, the Lower Swansea Valley
Project can only be counted a thorough-going success if
the Welsh Office, Swansea Corporation and the citizens of
Swansea themselves have the will and imagination to follow through.

Elsewhere in Britain they have precedents for action.
Though nothing quite so creative and comprehensive as
the Swansea blueprint has been followed, much less devised, elsewhere – and though in general the past record
of land renewal in Britain is disappointing – there are a
few local authorities, a few enlightened industries, and
more than a few voluntary groups who have been
appalled by the dereliction around them and have done

something about it. What these few activists have achieved should shame the inactive. Even more, what they have achieved demonstrates that it is by no means beyond man's faculties to cleanse his landscape of the filth and squalor which he himself created.

Lancashire Green

Some twenty years ago Lewis Mumford predicted that given the will a smirchy Lancashire could become a garden again, that it had been a terrific act of energy which made Lancashire the hole that it had become and that it would take something of the same energy to restore it. The garden vision was off target: there is no reason why muscular Lancashire should look like soft Surrey; its history and its pursuits are too different. Yet about fifteen years ago the county's planners concluded that there was no reason why Lancastrians need be reminded on their every journey, to work or to play, of what had once made them rich and strong, but which by the 1950s was clearly impoverishing and enfeebling their environment and their prospects.

Lancashire has sensibly concentrated on the worst areas first. Eight of its so far completed thirteen reclamation schemes have been within the North Makerfield town map area (see map), littered with 388 acres of spoil heaps, 15 acres of pits and 1,378 acres of miscellaneous industrial junk – in all 20 per cent of the town map area is *officially* derelict even today. The county planners began modestly in 1952 with a cosmetic treatment of a naked-sloped, flat-topped shale heap at Bickerstaffe Colliery, an eleven-acre, 60-foot-high eyesore ever since the colliery had closed twenty-two years previously. Bickerstaffe is now the home of some 15,000 trees – alders as high as twenty-four feet, corsican pines eighteen feet. The whole operation including land acquisition and fencing cost no more than would a small family car – £653.

By the mid-1950s the council had moved on to more defiant subjects. They tackled a miniature Lower Swansea Valley scene – Whalley's Basin,* near Wigan, a sour sink of mining subsidence, chemical wastes, foul little canal and all-purpose rubbish dump. The 38 acres were filled, levelled and grassed, the contractor using improvised bulldozers from discarded wartime tanks and 60,000 tons of spoil from a nearby iron forge for fill. (Which incidentally allowed the forge to expand later on to the ground long sterilized by its own wastes.) Today the basin (no longer in fact a basin) is a green oasis in an area where grey dominates, and it provides a running track, four football pitches, a cricket field and a bowling green. Few outsiders would select 'beautiful' as the proper adjective to describe it, but to the people who live round it and play on it, Lew Wallace's claim that 'beauty is altogether in the eye of the beholder' is very true. It gives pleasure and satisfies social needs far beyond the £17,000 it cost to do.†

The county's biggest completed project – both in terms of acreage (180) and cost (£56,000) – is at nearby Bryn Hall, once a loathsome mountainscape of spoil tips and an enormous and treacherous flash. A million tons of spoil were moved from those locally nicknamed 'Black Alps' and the site is now pasture trimmed with spinneys. This project was the first phase of what is to be Lancashire's most ambitious undertaking yet: the transformation of

*Well named, as are a number of the county's derelict sites which have been or are to be renewed: Moor Pit, Industrious Bee, Dangerous Corner, Stoney Lane, Foggs Fold, Low Hall, Careless Lane.

†An object lesson for Swansea Corporation?

an adjoining 312 acres at the abandoned Long Lane
Colliery. Work began in 1968 on a landscape distin-
guished by derelict water towers, loading gantries and
pithead baths blasted for anything saleable in them and
by spoil heaps gouged into bizarre shapes during the search
for marketable shale, and by the tremendous silhouettes
of three smouldering tips known as the Three Sisters.
These will not be flattened (and so offend Ian Nairn) but
planted and contoured into a landscape which by 1970
will provide an industrial estate, a school, open space and
twenty acres of housing. The cost – a hefty £550,000 – will
be more than regained by the council from the eventual
sale.

Lancashire is still, for all its dereliction, a wealthy
county: a rateable value of £80 million and an annual
county budget of £115 million. But that alone does not
explain its successes so far. The accomplishments are
not explained either by a planning staff of 250 including
a land-reclamation section under T. Mather – although
that helps – nor by a high-powered chief planning officer
(Aylmer Coates) – although that helps. The successes are
explained by an *enlightened* planning staff (nine of whom
devote most of their time to reclamation), a co-operative
council, and a determination to get on with the job
despite the apathy of many smaller authorities in the
county and the weakness of central government policy.
The county has been the nation's pioneer in land renewal,
certainly – as one of its planning staff puts it – 'the first
county to do reclamation as an environmental exercise'.
The county has been pragmatic: 'Let's have a go has been
our motto,' says the same planner. 'The longer you argue,
the longer you leave it, the more it will cost eventually.' *

* A part of this pragmatic approach is that in some instances the
planners have swapped derelict land for common land; houses are

Lancashire gives contractors flexible target dates, permitting them to move their heavy plant to reclamation projects in winter or other times of under-use and withdraw them temporarily when needed elsewhere. This cuts costs, as do the deals the county sometimes makes with owners of derelict sites, permitting them to extract saleable shale for a fixed period and so later selling the land to the council for a much-reduced figure. The county acquires the derelict sites, engineers them and manages them for a couple of years before, in most cases, handing over the redeemed acres to district councils.* This gives the county the control essential to successful reclamation.

If some of Lancashire's land renewal has been done 'on the cheap', if some of the end-results are not very imaginative, at least *it has been done*. In the still depressing dereliction of the Lancashire Coalfield, there are signs today of what reclaimed acres mean to people: housewives from council estates (their very houses sometimes built on reclaimed land) who used to push their prams across scenes of desolation and gossip at the dirty feet of colliery tips do this now on paths and benches on gently rolling green expanses; and on the fringes of some of these new green places, private builders have put up the kinds

---

built on the common land and the derelict land is reclaimed and becomes the new common. Ian Campbell, secretary of the Commons, Open Spaces and Footpaths Preservation Society, believes that such exchanges 'serve a very useful purpose and have often resulted in otherwise waste or derelict land being made into attractive open space'.

* Even so, some local councils don't want to – or argue that they can't – spend a penny and they fail to look after the reclaimed sites. Some of the county's reclaimed sites are now beginning to look tatty; a new dereliction born of apathy is creeping back.

of houses that have Jaguars in the garages. These things
– a lot of things – would not be happening but for land
reclamation.

Ironstone into Pastures

Today's sophisticated and powerful machines for tearing
minerals from the earth create bigger-than-ever messes;
yet they and other similar modern machines can ob-
literate their messes as once was never possible. Nowhere
has this been more obvious than in Britain's ironstone
fields of Lincolnshire, Leicestershire, Northamptonshire,
Oxfordshire and Rutland. Until the early years of this
century ironstone was excavated by hand at outcrops or
where the overburden was shallow. 'The topsoil was
usually stripped and wheeled in barrows to one side,' explains Northamptonshire's planning officer, Malcolm
Gregory. 'After the ironstone had been extracted, the
subsoil was returned and the topsoil spread evenly over
the area, so that cultivation of the land could quickly
follow.'

But the demand for iron and steel in the First World
War led to the development of mechanical diggers able to
exploit areas of deeper overburden, and an increasing
proportion of the land was left unrestored, in hills and
dales rising and falling as much as thirty feet – 'an unrelieved picture of devastation covering large tracts of
country', as Gregory describes it. Sometimes conifers were
planted, screening the dereliction but out of harmony
with the topography, and the dense scrub that grew up
in the man-made dales soon became breeding-grounds for
weeds and vermin.

This was the situation in 1939, when a government
committee regarded with 'but limited optimism' the pos-

sibility of agricultural restoration in the ironstone fields. But the rapid advance in earth-moving technology and – in this instance – firm government action proved the committee wrong. Machines got bigger and more ruinous, but they were capable of restoring as well as destroying. And in 1950, in a special order under the Town and Country Planning Act 1947, the government required ironstone extractors to strip and re-spread the topsoil. This order was confirmed and expanded a year later in the Mineral Workings Act which established the Ironstone Restoration Fund, the most sensible and far-seeing land-reclamation legislation so far devised.

Under this legislation, the producers are charged with restoration costs up to £110 per acre. Where reclamation exceeds this figure (£300 an acre or more is now quite common) they can draw on the fund, to which the ironstone owners and operators contribute $2\frac{1}{4}$d. and the Exchequer $\frac{3}{4}$d. per ton extracted. The fund has worked admirably. In Northamptonshire, where about a third of the total county – some 200,000 acres – is ore-bearing, the mineral companies have so far restored 3,600 acres since the 1951 Act and the county council has restored another 1,400 acres left derelict from pre-1951 days, the costs being re-imbursed from the fund. Nearly always the after-use has been for grazing.

There have been and still are some problems. The county council found that, with its long-standing dereliction, the topsoil had vanished and it was too expensive to transport from elsewhere. Though the planners re-claimed the land without topsoil, it has proved with the addition of fertilizers to be perfectly adequate pasture. At first the Ministry of Agriculture was unwilling to accept slopes finished to a gradient steeper than one in fifteen; eventually the ministry accepted a maximum of one in eight, which has presented no major obstacles to the free movement of farm machinery. The restored terrain does however present some problems of 'ponding' and special measures to improve drainage are needed – and paid for out of the fund. Also, to get at ironstone deposits usually means blasting through seams of limestone as thick as thirty-five feet; this results in huge chunks of rock which must be buried if farming is to succeed afterwards. Stones near the surface of the restored land must be hand-picked, a slow and fairly costly operation. Despite technology's wonders, a really suitable stone-picking machine has not yet been developed.

But these are relatively minor obstacles and ironstone extraction is on balance a model of how mineral producers should treat (and be required by government to treat) the land. In Northamptonshire, relations between the county planners and the ironstone extractors are excellent. Stewart and Lloyd, the county's biggest extractors, are co-operative and conscientious about the quality of their restoration work. While the life-span of an ironstone quarry may be anything from twenty to thirty years, and its area of consent more than 1,000 acres, in fact areas larger than sixty acres are seldom disfigured by a single quarry at any one time – and then not for more than two or three years. Farming continues until the moment extraction begins; farming resumes as soon as the land is restored after excavations end. Though narrow, the temporary scars are deep and fierce, the awesome draglines plunging through earth and blasted stone to reach a deep seam of red-brown ironstone.

To the layman the redeemed pastures are indistinguishable from those never disturbed for ironstone, except that, unfortunately, fences have usually replaced the hedgerows. Luckily, the overburden extracted during ironstone working 'bulks' – loosens up – by about a third, so that there is sufficient material to accomplish restoration without the expense and difficulties of importing additional fill. The land which has been restored without topsoil is seldom suitable for crops, but as Gregory sums up the 1,400 acres the council has restored for pasture: 'They've relieved 1,400 acres elsewhere for crops.' At the latest calculation, Northamptonshire had only 303 acres of dereliction – and all 303 justified restoration. If this happy situation could be repeated with other industries and throughout the nation, dereliction would not be worth writing about.

Restoration by Slurry — _mud._

One in every three tons of coal mined in Britain is burnt to produce electricity. A modern coal-fired power station consumes 20,000 tons of coal a day; it can produce a million tons of waste ash each year. Because of this, in the early 1960s at its great Trent Valley power stations, the Central Electricity Generating Board faced a crisis of what to do with its mountains of fuel ash. All available holes in the neighbourhood of the power stations had been filled and it was uneconomic to transport or pipe the ash to distant pits. 'If it had been fifty years ago,' says a board officer, 'we could have made bloody great piles outside the stations.' But public opinion, the 1957 Electricity Act, and the board's own amenity-consciousness ruled that out. The board examined dumping the ash in The Wash, but negotiations involved so many landowners that the scheme was rejected as too cumbersome.

Finally the board decided on the brick-clay field round Peterborough, some sixty miles from its major Trent Valley stations, a 1,000-acre industrial desert pockmarked by immense excavations. British Rail concluded that at eight or ten shillings a ton it would be profitable to transport the fuel ash in sealed waggons by a merry-go-round of trains running from power stations to pits. A remarkable exercise in land reclamation was about to begin.

The CEGB spent about £3.5 million on facilities to do the job, including a rail terminal capable of unloading forty-eight ash-filled waggons in seventy minutes. In 1966 the operation began, and since then, six days a week round the clock, up to seven trains a day, each loaded with 1,000 tons of ash, have trundled back and forth. The ash, transported in its pulverized dry form, is mixed with water and pumped straight into the pits as a thick wet slurry; there, in time, it 'cements' like volcanic ash, hardening to the point where it makes a suitable base for housing or industrial buildings. Alternatively topsoil can be spread over the ash-filled pits and farming resumed.*

So far the board has already filled one eight-acre pit. It is filling faster than the brick-makers are making new holes; even so it will take twenty years to fill the present holes – and in time the brick-makers will dig another 2,000 acres of holes. The present pits can swallow thirty million tons of fuel ash; if clay excavations continue as anticipated, fifty-two million tons will be needed to restore all the area.

It is an expensive project, and the electricity consumer is paying the bill. The brick-makers have the effrontery to not only charge the CEGB a few pennies for every

---

*To this end, the CEGB is stockpiling 10,000 tons of topsoil made available, gratefully, by the British Sugar Corporation at Peterborough, whose problem is a mountain of earth resulting from the washing of sugar beets. A fortuitous bit of co-ordination.

ton of ash pumped into their pits, but they also charge the board rental for the terminal buildings the C E G B itself built and paid for. And as the pits are restored, the brick companies will inherit the new land and sell it. About a quarter of the programmed restoration area at Peterborough will be occupied by an industrial estate; on that the brick-makers will make a fat profit.

But the C E G B, as one of its officers explains, 'is not in the land-reclamation business ... we're not Lady Bountiful'. The board's job is to produce electricity at the lowest possible cost, competitive with its rivals, gas and oil. The Peterborough scheme is solving a waste-disposal problem for the board; it is – as it happens – doing a piece of land reclamation on a vast scale. But it is also raising the price of electricity. Each time the electricity consumer turns on a switch, he is making his little contribution to the trading profits of the brick-makers.

The Peterborough project is, then, an example of land redemption that 'just happened' as the result of unusual circumstances, and the government and the local authority have been no more than spectators. In the late 1950s the electricity industry was expanding at the rate of eleven per cent a year: this resulted in more and more huge power stations, producing more and more ash. Growth has now slowed to seven per cent, and with the gradual movement by the C E G B away from coal to oil, natural gas, and nuclear power for firing its stations, and with the C E G B energetically selling more of its ash each year, the ash available for land reclamation will be limited * – even though the total amount of fuel ash

* Pulverized fuel ash is also a valuable raw material for the construction industries. The C E G B already sells about forty per cent of all its ash each year for the manufacture of building blocks, lightweight aggregate, stabilized roads and other things.

produced each year is expected to reach 15 million tons in the early 1970s. As G. A. W. Blackman, an assistant regional director of the C E G B, has warned: 'The generating board is not today in the position where it has millions of tons of ash lying around which is an embarrassment to us. In the days when we thought of Peterborough we had at all costs to find a very large field for what was then a liability.' Today the board would not consider so elaborate and expensive an operation. Without subsidies and incentives, a success on the scale of the Peterborough reclamation scheme will not be repeated elsewhere.

Creative Coalmining

The deep-mining section of the National Coal Board has a deplorable record of incessantly creating new dereliction and rarely restoring its past dereliction. This is due not only to the fact that deep-mining operations have lost more than £85 million over the past fifteen years – and so there simply isn't the money for reclamation – but also to what one observer with intimate experience of dealing with the deep mines section calls 'its conservative and autocratic attitudes'.

The opencast executive of the N C B, responsible for the production of between 6 and 7 million tons of coal per year, is a happy exception. Although it is charged by the government to restore its excavations, the opencast executive in recent years has gone beyond this requirement and harnessed exploitation of coal to creative reclamation of both its own and others' despoliation. This good record is due not only to the fact that the opencast operations have made a profit of more than £77 million over the past fifteen years but to an attitude of responsibility about the unavoidable disturbance to land and people caused by its operations. Since 1952, the opencast executive has restored more than 100,000 acres, which includes not only nearly all the dereliction created by its own operations but also the movement of some fifty huge spoil tips left by its deep-mining colleagues.

Because of the opencast executive's expertise in land renewal, the Minister of Housing has requested the executive to offer its services to local authorities contemplating reclamation projects. The executive has agreed and is doing so, although there has been no great rush by local authorities to accept the offer. For those authorities who do accept the services, the executive surveys their dereliction, investigates land ownership, prepares restoration plans and draws up the contracts. If the executive has a viable opencast operation in the area, it does not charge for these services, though by its agreement with the government it is entitled to. The executive encourages local authorities in development areas to apply for the eighty per cent grants; and though it has even offered to pay the remaining 15 per cent itself, this radical proposal alarmed the government. The Ministry of Housing claimed it would 'upset an accounting principle' – yet another example of bureaucracy positively stifling reclamation.

In the Harrow offices of the opencast executive there are vast maps which illustrate what the executive's director-general, F. C. Baker, calls 'our policy of concentrating on sites where we can do good ... getting at our coal in and around dereliction'. One set of maps plots the areas of derelict land from deep mining in Northumberland and County Durham; atop them are clear plastic maps plotting the opencast coal reserves in the same counties. On the basis of such maps, the executive offers to site its operations at the points where opencast reserves and high concentrations of dereliction coincide; at the end of its extractive operations – two or three years at any one site – the executive will sweep away the deep-mining mess in the process of restoring its own workings. The restored land is commonly returned to agriculture, although houses – if placed on raft foundations – can be built on it soon after restoration; after ten years, to allow for settling, they can be built without rafts.

This policy of co-ordinating extraction and renewal is so sensible and constructive that it is a particular pity that the government's fuel policy, announced in November 1967, puts future opencast operations in jeopardy, as part of the cutback in coal production in coming years. The opencast executive had hoped to mine nine million tons a year in future; it will be lucky to mine six, and some of its dramatic proposals * for co-ordinating extraction and restoration may not be realized.

Other Achievements

In Nottinghamshire, which spent £11,000 on reclamation in 1967–8 and which budgeted some sixty per cent more in 1968–9, the achievements so far include the reshaping and grassing of spoil heaps at Cossall Colliery, a fifty-acre eyesore which closed in 1967. The county has also revived a thirty-acre derelict site in Kirby-in-Ashfield, on which in 1965 grass was seeded hydraulically direct on to the shale tips and has thrived. Jack Lowe, the county planning officer, considers his greatest satisfaction to date to be 'the day we saw our first sheep grazing on it'.

In the West Riding, three obtrusive cones at the abandoned Mitchell Main Colliery have been reshaped and planted with grass and trees and the forty-four-acre site

* See Chapter 9.

now blends happily with the surrounding countryside. Four years ago the planning committee of the West Riding County Council set up a team in the planning department to look at the environment as a whole, with special reference to the deterring effects of industrial dereliction upon new industries and population. The team, under John Casson, has since grown from three to thirty members. Its recent successes include the face-lift and landscaping of a sixty-acre former colliery site alongside the M1 near Wakefield.

Among a number of restoration works in Staffordshire, the rehabilitation of eighteen acres of colliery dereliction at Wallbrook is imaginative. A housing estate was built on doubly reinforced concrete rafts, and a disused pit shaft was enlisted as a soakaway for the estate. Acquisition and levelling cost about £11,000 and the costs have been more than offset by the site values created by the renewal.

In 1964 County Durham established a reclamation team in its planning department; it now has eleven members. Its operations are geared to using the services of the NCB opencast executive and, when needed, outside consultants. Richard Atkinson, the county's planner, has had some success in encouraging the deep-mines section of the Coal Board at least to consult with him when they intend major extensions of existing tips under the *carte blanche* of the General Development Order. In some cases, as a result, topsoil has been salvaged for later restoration rather than simply overlaid with spoil; plans for conical heaps have been altered to more acceptable flat-topped ones; and the NCB has done some soiling and grassing of its tips. Reclamation has progressed slowly, but the county has started eighty reclamation schemes since 1965, covering 2,000 acres at a gross cost of about £2·5 million, the county council contributing £500,000 and the government £2 million. The county plans to deal with 500–600 acres a year in future, but even then, for all its successes, won't be able to keep up with the land becoming derelict through colliery closures.

In Newcastle, the university's department of town and country planning, in collaboration with the Ministry of Housing and local authorities in the North East, has set up a three-year reclamation project to investigate techniques of landscape design and treatment on six major derelict sites in Newcastle, County Durham and Northumberland.

Since 1907 in Cornwall, some 3,000 acres of land made derelict by copper and tin mining have been reclaimed, mainly for farming, and another 2,000 acres now justify treatment. The county has recently applied for grants for reclamation schemes at a number of sites, including one with a quite unusual after-use: a nine-acre gypsy caravan site near Camborne. And by imposing stringent planning conditions on the winning of stream tin in the Carnon Valley near Truro, a small and attractive lake district is being gradually created. H. W. J. Heck, the county planning officer, is however up against 'the cultural and sentimental value in some of the old tin-mining wastes ... a unique landscape and for many Cornishmen evocative of a past of which they are proud'. He is prepared to retain some of the old mines as open-air museums, but argues, 'There is still a tremendous amount that could be done to improve the quality of the environment and the earning capacity of the land.' Heck proposes, in Cornwall, a full-scale study of the problem 'along the lines of the Lower Swansea Valley Project'.

In Scotland, shale bings have been used successfully as

infill at the approach roads to the Forth Road Bridge and on site extensions to the B P oil refinery at Grangemouth. At Livingstone New Town, shale is being mixed with peat to create a major recreational area. At Westfield in Fife the opencast executive is reclaiming a 250-acre peat bog for agriculture and is creating a man-made loch as well. According to Fife's planning officer, Maurice Taylor, there are still 5,000 acres of derelict land in the county; hundreds have been reclaimed, including a thirty-seven-acre eyesore at Lochgelly, where derelict buildings have been demolished, pit shafts capped and bings regraded at a total cost of £36,200. It is now attractive and useful farmland. And in 1967 work began on the Lochore Meadows scheme in Fife, the largest rehabilitation project so far approved in Scotland. When completed in the mid 1970s at a cost of £1 million, the reclaimed four-square-mile area will include a country park, a recreational lake, and two industrial sites on the periphery of the area.

The county council of West Lothian has rehabilitated more than 200 acres over the past eight years for uses ranging from parkland to primary schools. Eric Hutton, the county planning officer, says that a £1 million land-renewal programme is now in progress and that 'the local authorities are well supported by the central government with eighty-five per cent grants'.

In Wales, stimulated by the formation of the three-man derelict-land unit in the Welsh Office in November 1966, there were sixteen separate reclamation schemes involving 360 acres and costing £812,000 during the unit's first year of operation. In the previous six years, only four schemes had been completed in all Wales. The unit's 1968 target was thirty schemes covering 1,499 acres at a cost of £1 million. The unit has even tackled some intransigent slate waste in Merionethshire, planting it with grass and trees. The unit proceeds in three steps, according to its senior executive officer, F. E. Brewer: first a member of the unit visits local authorities 'to get them interested'; then the unit inspects the derelict sites chosen for treatment by the local authority; finally, it advises and assists in the renewal schemes. Brewer admits he has encountered attitudes of 'Why pay for the legacy of the past?' He says that the answer is simple: 'If you don't, no one will.' He hopes the unit's work 'will be self-generating ... we're really salesmen'. The unit has had considerable success in overcoming apathy about dereliction, probably stronger in Wales than anywhere in Britain.

Voluntary Efforts

Elaborate and sometimes expensive successes like these require heavy plant and technical expertise. But in recent years a number of individuals and voluntary organizations throughout the derelict areas of Britain have been sufficiently outraged by the eyesores about them to do something more modest by way of a general tidying up, sometimes involving demolition of derelict buildings and planting of vegetation.

In the summer of 1965 teenagers at a Quaker work camp directed by Michael Graham of the Community Council of Lancashire, and financed by the Gulbenkian Foundation, grassed over and planted trees in spoil heaps near Atherton in Lancashire. Half of the twenty-two volunteers were foreign; there was only one representative from the local area – an all too frequent situation. Each Easter in recent years the Community Council of Lancashire has organized a short course in land improvement, combined with actual on-site work. Sixteen spoil tips in Lancashire, Cumberland, the West Riding and Nottinghamshire have been or are being terraced to prevent erosion (sometimes ponies are used to make the terraces on easier slopes, their hoof prints adequate for the job), and then planted. By using volunteers the improvement work has been done for only £20 an acre and when completed the sites are perfect for unorganized children's play.

The eyesores that are often left behind when the Forces evacuate lands so offended Michael Dower that about ten years ago, in Pembrokeshire, he organized voluntary work camps to clear unsightly military junk left behind on de-requisitioned airfields. He later brought the programme under the Civic Trust, and in all, until the scheme ended in 1962, eighty-five camps were run. 'We were trying to express our indignation,' says Dower, now director of the Dartington Research Trust. 'The government was responsible for making the mess, but not making sure of any tool to remove it.' *

Between November 1967 and May 1968 Operation Springclean – organized by the Civic Trust for the North West, the North West Economic Planning Council and other bodies – succeeded in brightening some of the dreary and derelict blotches on the region. Most of the 183 local authorities in the region co-operated; twelve towns cleared some of their derelict sites, many of the scars of the industrial revolution were at least camou-

*Very occasionally the Ministry of Defence does remove eyesores, either on its currently owned property or on de-requisitioned lands. The ministry is now clearing unsightly huts from Yatesbury in Wiltshire, a site sold to about 150 different purchasers on condition that they cleared the huts to ground level. They didn't. The land will ultimately be restored to agriculture. On its own land at Branston, Staffordshire, and Sculthorpe, Norfolk, the ministry is demolishing unsightly and dangerous buildings.

flaged, some of the 'Coronation Streets' in the old cotton and coal towns were brightened up a bit.* The campaign was successful enough for the Yorkshire and Humberside region to plan a similar springclean.

In November 1967 the Nottinghamshire Trust for Nature Conservation and the Council for Nature's Conservation Corps recruited hundred of volunteers, many of them schoolchildren, who under the supervision of the county's planning and forestry staffs planted in a single week 12,000 trees † supplied by the county council on a landscaped spoil tip at Newstead Colliery.

In January 1966 the Civic Trust for the North East established Youth Enterprise to channel volunteers to work on clearing industrial dereliction and generally improving the environment. The N C B seconded an employee to assist the project, and Malcolm Shepherd of Community Service Volunteers joined in. Among the principal Youth Enterprise projects in 1967: on four weekends young people from the Auckland area planted over 18,000 trees on disused gravel quarries alongside the River Wear; and a derelict sawmill and miscellaneous rubbish was cleared at Castle Eden Dene by seventy young people on a fortnight's camp.

A springclean of the eyesores in the Rhondda Valleys

---

*The only depressing thing about this operation was that the greatest stimulus for it was a visit by the Queen to the region in May 1968; much of the work done was 'window-dressing' and will quickly deteriorate. This is the sort of thing that often happens when Lord Robens makes his rounds of collieries: 'instant' landscaping appears, white paint is splashed about liberally, flower beds suddenly sprout up outside the works manager's office. A few weeks later everything is back to its black normal.

† This is a quarter as many trees as the London Brick Company (which likes to advertise the fact) has planted round its workings in all the years since the Second World War.

has been tackled for the past two years by Rhondda Youth Action, assisted by the Civic Trust for Wales, Community Service Volunteers and the Rhondda Borough Council. The group's most ambitious project has been the clearance and transformation of a derelict site in heavily populated Ynyshir into an adventure playground. Tunnels, bridges, barrels and tree trunks have been laid out instead of the usual swings and climbing frames – an imaginative project more in line with children's real play needs than the conventional playground. Work camps at Easter and in the summer have attracted thirty local young people and small teams from International Voluntary Service.

A similar and continuing campaign – but on canals – has been carried out in recent years by the Inland Waterways Association, a national voluntary organization concerned, as one member puts it, with 'the several hundred miles of inland navigation which are in various stages of decay'. On weekends volunteers have cleared banks on the River Wey preparatory to repairs by the National Trust; removed weeds and rubbish from the Peak Forest Canal; tidied locks and footpaths on the South Stratford Canal; and over three years restored Stourbridge Canal. The I W A admits that large-scale restoration of derelict canals cannot be completed entirely by volunteers. But their efforts chivvy local authorities with the money and machinery into action, and the voluntary work cuts the final costs of restoration of disused or decaying waterways.

Young volunteers like these have been called by the Civic Trust 'people who care enough about their surroundings to wield picks and shovels'. Caring enough is the key to all these successful examples of land redemption, whether for humble facelifting schemes by voluntary groups or million-pound projects by county councils that literally move mountains. Caring enough is what distinguishes councils and planning officers in those few areas where real drive has been applied to land renewal. Caring enough is what has urged on some enlightened industries to stop spoiling our landscape with their wastes. Caring enough is the first prerequisite to attacking the really stubborn dereliction that has so far been ignored or considered hopeless – and to preventing the even greater dereliction that threatens to spoil our environment tomorrow.

Chapter 9: The Future

> I have a gloomy foreboding that ... this generation
> will go down in history as one which cared about
> computers and cosmonauts, about sex and soccer, but
> not very much about creating civilized surroundings
> for people to live in.
>
> — RICHARD ATKINSON, county planning officer,
> Durham

THE coming decades are at once reassuring and cheerless for anyone earnestly concerned about man-made
dereliction in Britain. The future is reassuring in that a
number of large-scale reclamation schemes for the years
running up to the twenty-first century either have been
proposed and stand a tolerable chance of being realized
(the Lower Swansea Valley Project discussed above) or
have actually been adopted and got under way (the Lee
Valley Regional Park discussed below). The future is
cheerless for two reasons: there are no evident signs that
land renewal will outpace – or even keep pace with – new
dereliction; some enormous and seemingly intransigent
blots of dereliction appear (short of some very radical solutions) to be permanent disfigurements of our landscape.

The Hopeful

That literate angler Izaak Walton would not have recognized his rural Lee * River Valley when, in 1944, the late

* There has been considerable fribbling over spelling: the Civic
Trust favours 'Lea', the government 'Lee'. Since 'Lee' has been
adopted in the Act of Parliament establishing the park authority, it
would appear sensible to conform.

Sir Patrick Abercrombie's Greater London Plan spoke of the valley as 'an opportunity for a great piece of regenerative planning'. By then gravel workings, sewage plants, water works, factories and power stations were already pressing north from London into the valley, swallowing or scarring the green lands, the still-undeveloped pockets of open space amidst man's excrescences increasingly isolated, shrinking and slowly deteriorating. Abercrombie saw in the Lee Valley the perfect vehicle for his 'green wedge' concept of bringing fingers of countryside straight into the metropolis.

The idea lay fallow for nearly twenty years and the valley became more and more London's premier junkland. But in August 1961 the mayor of Hackney, concerned about the creeping dereliction on his borough's doorstep, took neighbouring local authority officers on an eye-opening boat trip along the Lee below Tottenham Lock. What they saw led finally, in April 1963, to a meeting of ten local authorities in the area at which the Civic Trust was invited to make a broad appraisal of rejuvenation of the valley. Later eight more local authorities joined and the reference area was extended to cover the whole of the lower Lee Valley from West Ham to Ware in Hertfordshire. On 20 July 1964 the Civic Trust submitted its plan. The Greater London Council, the counties of Essex and Hertfordshire, six London boroughs and six smaller authorities promoted a Bill in Parliament to set up a regional park authority to turn the area into a playground for the million Londoners who lived within two miles of the valley. The Lee Valley Regional Park Act received the Royal Assent on 21 December 1966.

The Civic Trust found nearly 6,000 acres of uncommitted land in the valley, which it described as 'London's kitchen garden, its well, its privy and its workshop ...

London's back door'. There were acres 'damp and derelict, unheeded and ill-kempt ... interwoven with factories and power stations ... a wilderness of gravel digging and its legacy of pits and derelict machinery ... the river harnessed, an industrial waterway, but still buildings stand derelict ... and weeds flourish on deserted land'. The trust proposed a chain of urban parks stretching more than twenty miles, turning the filter beds of abandoned water works into formal lakes and water gardens and pre-planning gravel digging to create new lakes: 'a series of water-parks to rival the Broads'.

Since the regional park authority was established on 1 January 1967 and despite the country's economic squeeze the first steps towards creating this vast linear playground have been taken. Throughout 1967 and 1968 the regional park authority has been gradually acquiring land and negotiating with gravel operators so that areas now in the course of extraction and yet to be extracted will be dealt with to conform with the ultimate plans for the valley. Work began in 1968 on a golf course at Picketts Lock near Enfield. The authority – consisting of elected representatives from the G L C, Hertfordshire, Essex and fifteen London boroughs and district councils – has established liaison with the Sports Council and regional sports councils. The West Ham College of Technology is co-operating with the authority on a survey of buildings of industrial–archaeological value, some of which may be preserved.

In the northern part of the 10,000-acre park the empha-sis will be on water-based activities, including the first Olympic standard rowing and canoeing course in Britain. In the southern part, there will be more urban-style recreational facilities, especially for younger people starved of open space in London's East End. The major development projects have a twelve- to fifteen-year target date; the rest could be completed within twenty years. The authority is aiming at the highest standards of architectural design, layout and landscaping and it hopes that the project 'will set the pattern and provide a prototype for similar schemes elsewhere and the reclamation of the many other Lee Valleys throughout Great Britain'. The project is the first practical example of the still controversial 'green wedge' * as opposed to green belt policy. If the Lee Valley project succeeds, it will be in fact, as the authority states, 'the first regional park planned for regeneration and rehabilitation as opposed to a national park which is usually an area of outstanding beauty preserved in its natural state'.

Three imaginative schemes have been advanced by Land Use Consultants for the opencast executive of the NCB, based on the very sane logic that 'increasing population and its growing demands on land have led to recognition of the need for conducting extractive operations in such a way that the land can afterwards become an asset rather than a liability'.

The most dramatic of the three schemes is along the broad arc of Druridge Bay in Northumberland, an unspoilt coast with a hinterland defaced by spoil heaps and incongruous industrial hardware, a physical and visual barrier between Newcastle and the area of outstanding natural beauty just north of Amble. The proposals include a parkway to be built over coal reserves after its extraction (enabling most of it to be constructed at no

---

* Some planners argue that it will be impossible to 'hold' green wedges in urban areas; under competing land pressures they will eventually coalesce. These critics consider that for all the bites that have and are being taken into the green belts around our cities, the belts are more tenable.

cost to ratepayers or taxpayers) and England's first seaside country park – of two to three square miles, to be built on the existing Coldrife opencast site. In all, the project would 'substitute a renewed landscape for both old and new scars'.

The two other projects – at Polesworth and Cannock near Birmingham – include shelter belts, artificial lakes and new land forms. The Polesworth project – drawn up after lengthy negotiations between the opencast executive, the West Midlands Sports Council and the various local authorities concerned – links opencast mining over the next twelve years with 'progressively converting the disturbed sites into one of the nation's most advanced and comprehensive regional outdoor sports centres.' It would also include a deep water supply reservoir, an aquatic nature reserve and field study centre, a parkway and large expanses of farmland. The Cannock scheme proposes harnessing opencast operations to the creation of 'a network of recreation corridors' in a ten-square-mile area, fitting in with renewal proposals of Staffordshire County Council.

Of course these projects are, in part, a public relations exercise. They are a carrot to local authorities to grant planning permissions for opencast workings. But they illustrate that *planned* exploitation of coal can help to meet the nation's growing recreational needs, much as, accidentally, the Norfolk Broads are the result of peat extraction in the Middle Ages. Hopeful though these three Coal Board projects are, the uncertain future of the coal industry casts some doubts on whether they will ever be realized.

In Scotland the Midlothian and West Lothian Joint Planning Advisory Committee and the Scottish Development Department have put forward a long-range rehabilitation plan for clearing derelict sites in or near urban areas, roads and airports. East Lothian County Council has prepared a six-year land-reclamation programme systematically to remove or contour and landscape the shale bings in the area, some of which are still burning. One bing has already been removed by the South of Scotland Electricity Board for use in construction of Cockenzie power station. The 1968–73 programme will renew nearly 300 acres at a total estimated cost of £316,150, providing woodland, shelter belts and recreational facilities.

Telford New Town in the Coalbrookdale district of east Shropshire will ultimately absorb and renew some 9,000 acres of dereliction. N. Bennett, the county planning officer, says that much of it will be given over to open space and amenity area.* Corby New Town in Northamptonshire will soon expand on to 600 acres of land once mined for ironstone. The new town corporation is building experimental housing on the site – some with special raft foundations, some without – to test whether there are any serious subsidence problems. Consultants advising on the expansion of Warrington in Lancashire have suggested development on 2,000 acres previously occupied by Risley Royal Ordnance Factory and Burtonwood Air Base, whose decaying buildings, hangars and sheds are classic examples of 'military dereliction'. With an estimated population growth in Britain that will require by the year 2000 the equivalent of another twenty cities the size of Birmingham or seventy the size of Newcastle, more new towns and more town expansions are

---

* There are, however, criticisms that the new town corporation is underestimating its provision of open space and that more derelict areas should be reclaimed now rather than later, when it will be a more expensive operation.

inevitable, concreting over more countryside. Other considerations of situation and transport-access satisfied, derelict land offers sites that would reduce the surrender of farmland and at the same time redeem scarred acres.

The Intractable

Probably the most obstinate, complex and sensational concentration of heaps and holes in the nation is the thirty square miles of china-clay tips and pits in Cornwall. Obstinate, for there seems no economic solution tomorrow, any more than today or yesterday. Complex, both because of the apparent immortality of the workings and because, as a valuable export to North America, china-clay exploitation raises that uncomfortable polarity of amenity versus dollars. Sensational, simply because such savage dereliction has a lunatic attraction. It may be that we should accept the lunatic and forget the rest. We may have no choice.

The local uses for china-clay waste – in building blocks, paving slabs and fencing posts – make little more impression on the gigantic heaps than a kiddy's toy shovel on the Cornwall beaches. London's construction industries *could* make an important impression, but there are no indications that the china-clay industry and British Rail can come together on a haulage price that would make the waste an economic proposition 240 miles away from its dumping ground.

The county planner, H. W. J. Heck, appears resigned to living with his mess of clay. He says: 'It is generally accepted that there must be large areas to the north of St Austell where the claims of the industry are given priority over all other forms of land use.' He would, however, like to see the official government definition of derelict land 'widened to include land which is unused for more than say ten years'. When the county council became the planning authority some twenty years ago, china clay companies applied for and were often granted planning permissions on land which they had no intention of immediately exploiting, but on which they wished to establish prior claims for the future. Often such land remains untouched even today – it is not ripped apart, but is totally neglected and so presents eyesores of a different order. 'An official recognition that such areas also require treatment could strengthen the position of the planning authority in its approach to the companies to see whether a phased scheme of reclamation could be agreed,' says Heck.

There is at least one bright spot in all this. In recent years, china-clay extractors have taken to disposing of their waste by conveyor belt and heavy lorry, producing low elongated tips instead of the conical tips once so characteristic of Cornwall. These can be more easily vegetated and, explains Heck, 'This more flexible method [of disposal] offers exciting possibilities of land sculpture.' But he immediately adds: 'As the whole landscape in the china-clay area ... is constantly changing, one wonders if there is any real justification for insisting on landscaping or reclamation for agriculture at this stage.'

In October 1967, Geoffrey Cowley, Bedfordshire's planning officer, published a planning appraisal of the Fletton brickfield in his county. In January 1968 he organized a conference of all interested parties, ranging from conservationists to the brick-makers themselves, to examine ideas for rehabilitating the 1,400 acres dominated by 'the batteries of tall chimneys, the gaping holes of active and derelict clay workings ... all in all a depressing experience'. At the conference J. P. Bristow, deputy chairman of the London Brick Company, described the same area as 'a scene of intense industrial activity in a country which lives by industry; we don't find it depressing'. These contraposed views underlined the intractability of the Bedfordshire brickfield problem, the working areas growing by 43 acres a year and due eventually to blot nearly 4,500 acres of land.

The national economic importance of the clay field is incontestable and it is no good being too soft-boiled: the clay must be worked. One in every five new houses in Britain is built with bricks from the Bedfordshire field. The peculiar characteristics of the clay there make the field the more valuable. The so-called 'fletton knotts' of clay have a twenty per cent moisture content and when ground into a consistent size they can be pressed into bricks which can be fired immediately, without the long weathering process of conventional bricks. The knotts have a ten per cent carbonaceous content which reduces the amount of fuel usually required for firing by about two thirds. The brickfield is also important for the local economy. It employs thousands of men * and the London Brick Company alone (and there are two other major firms working the field) pays about £150,000 a year in rates – the fact of which the company unsubtly reminds county planners when they object to its rape of the landscape.

The thick and valuable grey-green clay knotts occur at depths averaging fifty feet; topsoil, subsoil, seams of brown clay called 'callow' and wet non-carbonaceous blue clay are rejected, resulting finally in vast 'knottholes' as deep as 100 feet, their bottoms ribbed with grotesque conical hills. With nearly 100 million cubic yards of holes already,

---

* Because of the arduous and unpleasant nature of the work, a high proportion of the workers are immigrants; in the 1950s and early 1960s, mainly Italians, now mainly Indians and Pakistanis.

the problem of finding filling appears insuperable, and the ambiguous restoration conditions imposed on the brick-makers by the government cannot anyway be enforced. The brick-makers have and are doing some infilling themselves, but not to any thought-out programme of land reclamation. In fact, simply because it is a convenient hole for their operations, they are filling a derelict 245-acre water-filled pit known locally as Stewartby Lake which could be transformed into a first-class recreational lake in an area short of water for leisure. The brick-makers won't entertain the idea, for fear the traffic of pleasure seekers might interfere with their operations; what could be a socially valuable amenity is fenced off and ringed by KEEP OUT signs. Other pits are being used for town-refuse tipping by local authorities, but the quantities are too small for any wholesale restoration. Bedford Corporation, using controlled tipping, dumps 200,000 cubic yards of refuse a year – and pays £950 annually for the privilege.*

For the Bedfordshire pits, so obviously visual deficits, are considered by Bristow as 'one of our assets'. At the brickfield conference one critic of this attitude described it as 'like a pickpocket selling back the wallet after he has emptied it'. Not only do the brick-makers have no intention of stopping charges on those who in effect are contributing to fulfilling the supposed restoration conditions 'imposed' on the brick-makers, but as Bristow argues, 'Any suggestion that the companies should contribute to the cost of refilling can only mean an increase in the price of

---

* The county negotiated for some time with the G L C, in the hope that London's monumental rubbish could be transported to fill the pits. After a feasibility-study of rail transport of refuse, the G L C concluded that incineration in London was more economic, and the hopes collapsed.

bricks at a time when profit margins are already being eroded by ever-increasing costs.* How could we then compete with all the materials new and old which flood the market?' Inadvertently, he has betrayed the brick-makers' fears: it is an old-fashioned product; a house laboriously put together with 18,000 separate slabs of fired clay is really archaic in an age of concrete and plastics and industrialized building.

For the immediate future, however, the brickfield seems destined to be a battlefield of craters and callow heaps, fierce chimneys (111 of them in all) spouting foul plumes, noxious smells in the air, trees mutilated by pollution into thalidomide shapes. The only serious proposal for restoration (apart from the unsuccessful idea of GLC refuse) has come from Nottinghamshire, which would like to mount a Peterborough-style merry-go-round of trains to move between three and four million tons of coal spoil now defacing 2,500 acres of the county to the brick pits each year, thus reclaiming vast tracts in both counties. (Unless some drastic remedy is applied, another 7,000 acres of Nottinghamshire will be overlaid with spoil heaps by the end of the century.) But this idea has foundered on finances: British Rail is asking a prohibitive 14s. 6d. a ton to move the spoil the 90 miles from Mansfield to the brickfield. Even if an economic price could be agreed – and it is estimated that at the present rate quoted by British Rail it would cost about £4 million a year for twenty years to fill the holes – the physical operation

---

* And, in his annual report to shareholders, in May 1968, the firm's chairman, Sir Ronald Stewart, boasted that the company grows in its own nursery 1,000 trees a year (the number of trees one trained forester could plant in one day) and concluded his defence of the company's attitude by saying: 'We could hardly, therefore, be accused of doing nothing.'

would be staggering. As a Ministry of Agriculture officer explained at the brickfield conference: 'To fill the holes material would have to be delivered at the rate of twenty train loads a day, each train carrying 1,000 cubic yards, six days a week from now until the year 2000.' To do it in twenty years would mean a yet larger operation.

At the conference Cowley urged the government to set up an advisory committee on the problem. There has been no progress on this, and the comments at the conference by Niall MacDermot, then Minister of State at the Ministry of Housing, summed up the apparent hopelessness of the situation and the government's lack of enthusiasm to be involved in a solution. 'I hope that no one is going to leap to the conclusion that my presence means that the government is about to wave a magic wand at the expense of the taxpayer in order to solve all these problems.'

Among the many other proposals for future reclamation which appear unhopeful, the barbarous business on the Durham beaches is outstanding. Since 1919 the coal industry has been dumping more than a million tons of spoil each year over the cliffs and on to a six-mile-wide beach which, punningly if pathetically, might otherwise be called 'unspoilt'. And not only coal dust and pit stones, but old rubber belting, scrap metal and pit timber is spilled on to the sands, described by the county planner as 'indescribably filthy'. The actions of the sea distribute the foulness far south of the dumping grounds. A coastal survey in 1966 resulted in two alternative suggestions: barging the waste to sea, or crushing it and depositing it in at least 100 feet of water. (There are no suitable holes near the collieries.) The county argues that either alternative is practical and economic; the Coal Board argues that either would be prohibitively dear; the government just watches the quarrel; the scandal continues and appears it will do so until the day the pits are shut down.

More than 3,000 acres of the West Riding's dereliction lies within sight of the future national motorways system planned for the county. At a motorways conference in July 1967, John Casson spoke of the despoliation in the corridors of the proposed motorways 'which by its very contrast with the bright modern ribbon of the motorway must seal an "image" with profound repercussions on [the area's] economic prospects'.*

Before the credit squeeze, West Riding proposed to landscape the M1 corridor, renewing 1,750 acres of derelict or degraded land at a cost of less than £250 per acre or £5,000 per mile of motorway. The total cost of land reclamation would have been less than the cost of a quarter-mile of motorway. A similar scheme was advanced to clean up and landscape 1,500 acres of dereliction along the programmed M62 motorway. An incidental but not unimportant social benefit of trees along the motorways would have been the considerable noise reduction. But the squeeze and the government's one-year ban on grants for 'green schemes' has meant that the opportunity for landscaping the M1 corridor may now have been lost for good; the motorway is too far advanced to take advantage of using the heavy road-building machinery on site and so doing the land redemption at an economic price. There may still be hope for the M62 proposal – *if* the government responds with uncommon swiftness to the county's plea.

* By contrast, the line of the completed M6 through Lancashire ingeniously avoids all areas of major industrial dereliction and presents the passing motorist with an image of a green and rural Lancashire, the horrific despoliation always just out of sight. It may well be that Lancashire's persuasive and highly capable surveyor, James Drake, had much to do with contriving this masterpiece.

An elaborate facelift of the Rhondda Valleys in Wales, proposed by the Civic Trust in April 1965, appears little more hopeful. The proposals to sweep away the legacy of 'carelessness, neglect, ruthlessness and indifference ... the scars and eyesores and the wastelands small and large' included an imaginative civic centre to be built on derelict land at Porth. It would incorporate housing, a hillside amphitheatre for 10,000, and a 'living museum of mining'. The proposals have collided with the squeeze, with monumental indifference, and with technical problems of communication and transport of materials and machinery in the isolated valleys. This admirable project is probably altogether too adventurous and elaborate and except for the gradual reclamation of spoil tips by local authorities, chivvied by the Welsh Office's derelict-land unit, and the modest clean-up campaigns by voluntary groups, it does not look as if anything dramatic is going to happen in the Rhondda.

Foreign Experiences

In our future actions on land renewal, we have before us the lessons of foreign nations. These are sometimes consoling, at other times disquieting. They show that for all the insufficiency of our efforts, we have taken reclamation more seriously than many countries – notably the United States. They also show that other countries – notably West Germany – have generally showed greater determination and a clear policy in recovering their squandered acres.

The Ruhr produces half of the Common Market's coal and a third of its steel. Nearly six million people live in the heavily industrialized 1,750 square miles overseen by the Ruhr Planning Authority, established in 1920 as the world's first regional authority of its kind. It grew out of a government commission in 1910 set up to prepare an open space plan for the Ruhr, and among the authority's numerous powers has been a continuous involvement in environmental preservation and improvement. One of the authority's first acts was to produce a master plan of the area, showing future land use and permitted developments. An independent and largely autonomous body, with real powers, the authority has since then established an excellent record of reclamation of dereliction, as well as prevention of new industrial encroachments on recreational areas. As Lord Robens has admitted, in the Ruhr the onus is on the mineral operator not to despoil the landscape and to produce a workable plan of after-use. According to C. J. Vyle, this requirement has resulted in a high quality of reclamation within the overall landscape plans for the region.

Today no less than thirty-eight per cent of the Ruhr planning area is given over to open space. Norman Perry notes that on average the cities of the Ruhr have more than eight times as much woodland per head of population as London. The authority has pursued the 'green wedge' concept – both to bring the countryside into the built-up areas and to trap and filter industrial air pollutants – and the wedges are often linked with the afforestation of spoil tips and the reclamation of other dereliction. Says Perry: 'The wedges help to fulfil the ideal of Ruhr planners, that its citizens should be able to walk right through the area from south to north.' Norman Pounds has written that no place within the industrial areas is more than six miles from open country and all the larger cities have extensive public woodland at their gates.

On a visit to the Ruhr when he was director of the Lower Swansea Valley Project, Kenneth Hilton noted the fast and progressive landscaping of spoil heaps: 'Conical tipping is avoided and when hogsback tipping extends far enough from the tipping face, the tip is planted progressively, leaving the minimum spoil area exposed to view.' Industrialists bear most of the cost of landscaping their own works and, said Hilton, 'take some pride in tackling the ugliness of the environment of heavy industry'.* If the same could be said of the deep-mines section of the N C B, some sectors of the cement industry and the brickmakers, many of our problems would be solved.

There are, however, some flaws in this happy picture. Pounds explains that in the Ruhr first-class farmland is often developed for industry or housing if it is conveniently sited, rather than unproductive, gravel-covered land in a somewhat less suitable location. He considers Britain's practice superior on this count. Hilton felt that the Ruhr had been less effective than Britain in controlling some forms of air pollution. Perry says that under an 1865 law, a mining firm whose activities cause land subsidence is required to pay compensation – and this obligation continues even after exploitation of the pit has ceased. This seemingly enlightened law has however led to mining firms buying up all the land which might be affected, thus either sterilizing it by withholding it from the market and keeping it as farmland, or allowing it to become derelict.

But on balance the accomplishments of the Ruhr planning Authority provide an example of co-ordinated and planned land reclamation from which we could learn much. The existence of a strong regional body has

---

*Hilton also noted the concern German Railways shows for landscaping embankments in industrial areas. It has a department responsible for planting trees and shrubs on embankments and a staff of landscape architects involved in improving the wider view for rail travellers. A lesson for British Rail.

eliminated, as Hilton put it, 'the rigid frontiers of authority that exist in Britain'. The authority has provided a *continuity* of environmental control for nearly half a century. Unlike the anaemic regional planning councils in Britain, the Ruhr authority has been given the powers and the money to deal comprehensively with the land on a regional basis.

Elsewhere in West Germany there have been admirable reclamation projects. Vyle cites one of the best: reclaimed gravel workings near Hamburg, resulting in a 600-acre complex of forests within which weekend houses and caravans have been sited, as well as restaurants, bathing strand, and boating and fishing facilities. Wilhelm Knabe has complimented the land-renewal work in the brown coal district near Cologne, where there is a special planning commission which ensures that opencast operations (in an area with deposits estimated at 60,000 million tons) are pre-planned. 'This planning includes reclamation right from the beginning,' according to Knabe.

In the Netherlands, where half of the country's land is subject to planned landscape development, the Dutch State Mines in the southern province of Limburg have a record of landscaping that should shame the N C B; the spoil tips are planted progressively and are black blots on the landscape for the briefest possible time. Once they are green they are – on Holland's flat landscape – attractive features. Rehabilitation and restraints on use have been applied to the Dutch coastal sand-dunes devastated by man – particularly by German bunkers during the Nazi occupation and by recreational use since. And of course Holland's record of men making land is stupendous; anyone who suggested in Holland (as is sometimes suggested in Britain) that man lacks the ability and the machinery to move the landscape to meet his needs would be laughed out of the country. As long ago as 1860 the Dutch reclaimed a polder, excavated for peat, covering 45,000 acres; since the sixteenth century the Netherlands has reclaimed 350,000 acres by draining lakes.

Mining operations in the Witwatersrand goldfield in South Africa during the past seventy years have resulted in golden-coloured waste dumps covering more than 25,000 acres; the dumps, consisting of finely ground rock from which gold and sometimes uranium have been removed, may reach 200 feet and a single one cover 100 acres. They are subject to severe erosion. The goldfield is also marked by huge flat-topped 'slime dams' – wastes suspended in water and piped to dumping areas – which may be 100 feet high and as much as 400 acres on top. Vegetation has now been established on the dumps and slime dams along a ninety-mile belt in the Witwatersrand, using a 'cocktail' of seeds of many grasses; some of them grow and die quickly, providing a humus, some provide nitrogen for other grass species, others provide tough and enduring vegetation. There was no physical way to stabilize the dumps, but vegetation has succeeded in doing it, stopping erosion by air and water and bringing green back into the goldfield wastelands.

The United States has failed lamentably at land-use. With some sixteen times more acreage per head than in Britain, America has long been profligate with land. A frontier philosophy – more open space always available over the next mountain – has ruled planners until quite recently. But in March 1968 the then President Lyndon Johnson asked Congress for a 100 per cent increase in funds for conservation measures 'to renew, to restore, to reclaim, and to refresh' the land. The thesaurus of synonyms was typical of Americans' lingual elaboration, and the funds he asked for were typical of America's

monetary luxuriance: $1,200,000,000 for the programme
in the year beginning 1 July 1968.

America's industrial dereliction is also on a scale, both
in expanse and the exotic, which makes Britain's problem
seem insignificant. In the Appalachians alone, and solely
as a result of coal mining, more than 800,000 acres of land
have been torn apart, and only a third of it so far reclaimed. Landscapes are gouged, hills ripped, whole ranges
of man-made waste-mountains spilled on the earth without a moment's conscience-prick. Opencast copper mines,
acid mine-water waste, contour strip mining, gold dredging, hydraulic mining for gold, borax pits – all these and
other earth-shattering activities prompted the then Secretary of the Interior, Stewart Udall, to survey the nation's
dereliction and in a report to the country in 1967 he
estimated that surface mining had already devastated
3.2 million acres (an area equal to all of Northern Ireland)
and that two million acres of it could be reclaimed – at a
cost of $757 million. By 1980, he said, more than five
million acres would be derelict. He asked that priority be
given to preventing future dereliction, and he tardily
warned the nation: 'We have looted and ravished the
land . . . the history of mankind is replete with civilizations
which tried to wrest from the land whatever was desired,
without regard to consequences.'

Tomorrow's Threats

Though on balance the past and present experiences of
other nations may console more than shame us, any com-
placency would be both unwise and arrogant. Particularly
when we examine what, unless we prevent it, will be tomorrow's dereliction in Britain. If our reclamation
doesn't quicken, by the year 2000 we shall have, by the

narrow official definition, at least 120,000 *more* acres of industrial dereliction than we have today. And this does not allow for the inevitable growth of nearly all the extractive industries apart from coal, nor for the development of more devastating extractive machinery making yet bigger heaps and holes, nor for the need for mineral operators to exploit thinner and less accessible seams and so throwing up yet more wastes, nor for the development of new industries with new manners of despoiling the landscape. As the Civic Trust has seen the future:

> Whether we like it or not, we are committed to an increasingly widespread exploitation of our mineral resources. In a competitive world, our survival as an industrial economy depends on it. We cannot prevent a continuing increase in our acreage of economically unfillable holes and immovable heaps.

The first statement is right; the second is alarmingly despondent and need not be right.

Yet the predictions of future damage do not encourage. There are already more than 1,350 sand and gravel pits in the country; there will be many more as production climbs to 170 million tons a year in the mid 1970s. John Taylor of Associated Portland Cement Manufacturers estimates that another 172,500 acres of gravel-bearing land will be required to meet the nation's needs before 1980. Many of tomorrow's gravel pits will be completely restored (some 300 already have been) and many wet pits will be turned into valuable recreational lakes (more than 5,500 acres of pits in twenty-seven counties are already so used). On balance the sand and gravel industry – with the exception of a few companies contemptuous of the environment – has a creditable record of land redemption. Yet the sheer size of future operations means that much more land will be scarred by active workings. This also means that there will be more derelict pits to deal with – even if the same proportion as in the past are restored or turned to leisure uses.

Ever greater quantities of wastes will be produced by the fast-expanding chemical industries. The Association of Public Health Inspectors has already expressed concern, on health grounds, about the often careless disposal of solid toxic wastes by subcontractors used by industry for the job. The carelessness and total disregard for the environment too common to such operators can also result in large areas of land soured by foul and dangerous wastes. This is a problem bound to become more critical in coming years.

The APHI also notes that despite the fast growth of the sand and gravel industry, many urban authorities have already filled all suitable nearby holes with town refuse. With trade and house refuse expected to increase over the next twenty years from its present 14 million to at least 22 million tons a year, there is a real danger that smaller authorities, without the resources or equipment to incinerate or otherwise process refuse, will create new and noxious wastelands near towns.

Natural gas is already revolutionizing the energy industry. Here the future picture is more encouraging. The Gas Council says that the problem of waste disposal at the country's two natural gas terminals – Easington in Yorkshire, and Bacton in Norfolk – 'is very small indeed, consisting largely of a relatively small amount of liquid hydrocarbons, which are transported by road tankers to other parts of the country. There is however a minor sulphur removal and recovery problem associated with one of the gas fields but even so the content of sulphur involved is relatively small.' As a result of the discovery and now the exploitation of natural gas, the Gas Council is 'not proposing to build any new gas works and in fact most of those already in action will be phased out of production in the next ten years or so.' A gas works typically occupies up to sixty acres, if an old-fashioned type, and about ten acres, if a modern type. We shall have to watch that these large works, as they are 'phased out', do not leave us with very ugly blots on our landscape.

The most controversial of tomorrow's threats to the landscape is atomic energy. By 1972 there will be twelve nuclear power stations in the United Kingdom, including three giants of 1,250 megawatts. Lord Robens has urged that nuclear reactors be sited underground, warning that above-ground reactors, when exhausted, will have to remain where they are 1,000 years or more, 'so leaving future generations with a number of permanent scars for which there is no remedy'. And at the Clean Air Conference in October 1967, a Coal Board officer, F. E. Schumacher, alarmed delegates about the danger of radioactive wastes from nuclear stations.

On examination both these warnings fail to stand up, perhaps motivated more by the N C B's fears of nuclear power replacing coal than by realities. Nuclear stations must be sited near cooling water, the national grid and on ground able to bear massive structures. These exacting requirements, according to G. R. Bainbridge, create a strong incentive to re-use the same or adjacent sites for future stations rather than new areas. An artist's impression in the magazine *Atom* of how Calder Hall would appear when its lifespan * is ended and the site reclaimed shows four mounds, each fifty to a hundred feet high, over the central region of reactors; everything else has been demolished and the whole site grassed or planted

---

* For accounting purposes a reactor's life is twenty years, but it may be closer to forty or even fifty in practice.

over with trees and freely accessible to the public. This, of course, is only an artist's impression; Calder Hall, and other reactors, when exhausted may not in practice be treated with so much concern for the environment.

The United Kingdom Atomic Energy Authority admits that the reactors themselves will have to be sealed off 'for several decades' and that it would be prohibitively expensive and technically difficult to remove the huge reinforced concrete and steel structures. The authority also admits that highly active wastes will have to be stored 'for generations'. (Low-active wastes are dispersed to sea or as effluent into rivers, under strict supervision by the government.) Laboratory wastes such as broken glassware and paper, which may contain slight contamination, are buried in trenches and earthed over; the authority says that such land could be used for other purposes 'in due course'. All highly active wastes are now stored at Windscale in Cumberland in stainless steel tanks, but they sterilize very small areas. Sir Roger Makins has said that 'the fission products arising from a year's processing of the fuel associated with 6,000 megawatts of nuclear generation can be safely accommodated in a tank thirty-five feet long times ten feet in diameter ... any fears that the storage of highly active wastes involves the spoliation of the countryside can be set at rest'.

The notion that tomorrow's landscape will be littered by unsightly, unapproachable and dangerous hulks of worn-out reactors appears then exaggerated. But, as with North Sea gas and new chemical industries bound to expand dramatically in decades to come, we must watch carefully that they do not despoil the land in the manner of their nineteenth-century predecessors.

For the remaining years of this century coal, as in the century past, will continue to be our major spoiler of land.

This despite a national fuel policy which anticipates coal production falling off from about 150 million tons in 1970 to 120 million in 1975. In May 1968 there were 374 active collieries in the country; another 70 were closed by March 1969. A greater proportion of the 'economic' pits which will remain will be the modern, mechanized ones which produce relatively more muck. Also, the closure of uneconomic pits in the North West, Scotland, Wales, Durham, Nottinghamshire and Kent is presenting and will present planning officers with vast areas of 'instant dereliction'. Though the spoil tips will no longer grow, the abandoned tips and colliery junk create overnight monumental restoration problems. These can be solved in time.

But they will not be solved unless Britain wakens fully to its disgrace of dereliction and mounts immediately a clean land operation to remove the detritus of past industrial activities and to prevent future degradations of the land. We may tomorrow become richer in money terms, but as the Civic Trust has put it: 'Advance in material well-being will be of little benefit if future generations are condemned to live amidst dirt, rubbish and dereliction.'

Chapter 10: The Solutions

Planned reclamation of derelict land on a comprehensive basis could have nearly as much impact on
the countryside in the next century as the creation of
country parks and estates in the eighteenth and nineteenth centuries has had on this.

– The Countryside in 1970, second conference, 1965

THE elimination of derelict land is not near the top of
the nation's priorities (and that is one of the troubles)
when considered beside the elimination of unemployment,
slum housing, poverty. Yet these higher-priority problems
are often corollaries of dereliction. By reviving the sick
lands of industrial dereliction – if the revival is done in
the wider context of area rejuvenation – we can contribute
to solutions of those more urgent problems. Degradation
of the environment radiates from the concentrations
of industrial despoliation. Very gloomy rays, depressing the landscape beyond the strictly derelict acres,
deadening the interstices between one blot of dereliction
and the next. Rehabilitation of those blots can lead to
rehabilitation of the areas around them. New housing,
new industry, new jobs can themselves radiate from the
revival of derelict lands.

There are no easy solutions, yet the redemption of
what may be as many as 250,000 acres disfigured by man
can be accomplished and in the long term can pay for
itself in social and even economic benefits. We already
have all the essential facts and technical capabilities to
act. Shouts – more often, murmurs – for more facts, more
research, more committees 'to look into the problem' are

simply delaying tactics. What we need now is the legislation, the organization, the money, the defined objectives and, most of all, the will to do the job.

The Legislation

What is required first is legislation to end the pollution of the land, along the lines of the laws we already have on pollution of the air and the water. Ideally, a Clean Land Act * would create a strong national land-reclamation agency with a fixed budget, sufficiently generous and guaranteed on a long-term basis. The act's goal should be a ten-, or, at most, twenty-year campaign as determinedly organized as a military operation. Local planning authorities should prominently participate in the organization and for a start should be required by the act accurately to survey all – not simply 'official' – dereliction within their boundaries. These surveys would include abandoned military lands and disused railways; land now being damaged by 'development' (such as waste tipping) which escapes planning control; land now in industrial use which does not have to be restored when use ceases; and land on which planning conditions imposed in the past have been inadequate or incapable of fulfilment. This means that a Clean Land Act will establish at the outset a realistic definition of derelict land.

Secondly, the act should require local planning authorities to produce – on the basis of those surveys – detailed blueprints for reclamation within the context of their overall development plans. A reasonable maximum time limit should be imposed for the surveys and the blueprints. And thirdly, local authorities should under

* I am indebted to Derek Senior for suggesting this neat and sensible title.

the act be compelled to clear away or clean up their industrial badlands, with target acreages and priority areas set by the national agency in which they will be represented.

With the exception of the Mineral Workings Act 1951, which set up the Ironstone Reclamation Fund, past legislation on land redemption has been inadequate. The Slagheaps Bill tabled in Parliament in 1966 was well-meaning but hastily drawn up and superficial, and it did not win government support. The bill to become the Clean Land Act must not suffer these weaknesses. It must be thoroughly thought out and expertly drafted. It must be comprehensive, concerned with all forms of man-made dereliction. It must have government support – indeed, it should properly be initiated by the government itself.*

The legislation must create a workable machinery that involves actively all interested parties and that reconciles reclamation with industrial activities essential to the nation's economy. It must however end the gutless surrender to industry that has been characteristic of both central and local government in the past. It must enlist the participation of enlightened industries in a national land-reclamation agency and, if need be, compel the unenlightened to co-operate or be penalized until co-operation becomes economically preferable to obstruction or inaction – the £ s d argument which may be the only one they can appreciate. By the incentives of a far more liberal grants system, reclamation must become positively advantageous rather than, as in the past, optional and

---

* But as we have seen in recent years, the government tends to leave the initiation of important social reforms (e.g. abortion, divorce) to private members. And redemption of derelict lands is as much a social as an economic undertaking.

questionable. The legislation must show that reclamation pays in all ways: economic, social, aesthetic.

The Organization

There are many structural prototypes for a national land-reclamation agency; if none has precisely the structure that would be required, they do at least provide some valuable pointers. The Ruhr Planning Authority is strong, well-equipped, adequately financed, capable of continuous and co-ordinated control over the clearance of dereliction. The Ministry of Transport's regional motorway-construction units have many of the powers and in some ways the structure that would be required by a land-reclamation agency. The structures of the New Town corporations provide some ideas, as does the consortium of planning officers in the Yorkshire and Humberside region. The Welsh Office's derelict land unit has some characteristics which might be expanded on a national basis. If our ill-conceived regional economic planning councils and boards had been given some executive rather than only advisory powers they might well have formed the framework for a national land agency. In any event, a regional approach to land redemption will be required by the agency; perhaps the present regions are about the right size and certainly the existing regional councils should be involved in the clean-land campaign. But since there is no possibility that a national agency could be set up under a Clean Land Act before 1971 at the very earliest, the practical results of the royal commissions on local government should be apparent by then and might suggest, or even dictate, the right shape and constitution of the agency.

The agency should be as independent and autonomous

as possible, though under the wing of a government ministry – in, perhaps, the manner of the National Board for Prices and Incomes – or at least under a larger and more influential body than itself. The Ministry of Land and Natural Resources, born then butchered almost immediately by the Labour government, would have been the appropriate ministry. Now the Ministry of Housing would seem the obvious choice, although its past record of lukewarm interest in land reclamation is not promising. The important thing is that only one ministry should have ultimate control over the agency. In the past too many government departments – Housing, Agriculture, Power, Transport, Public Building and Works, Board of Trade – have made sometimes conflicting decisions which directly or obliquely affected land reclamation. A national land agency under a single ministry must be able to know those decisions in advance of their execution, so as to tie them in with land renewal. A possible overseer might be Kenneth Robinson, appointed in 1968 Minister for Planning and Land.

There are other possible homes for a national land agency. There is the Civic Trust, but it lacks the staff for the job and might not comfortably absorb the new bodies required. It is better equipped for tidying up eyesores than for vast reclamation projects. It is more an 'ideas shop' and a prod to others than a practical operational body, and the fact that the trust is financed by industry might muffle the strong hand that must be applied to compel industry to co-operate in land redemption. The Land Commission, with headquarters in Newcastle and eleven regional offices (including Cardiff and Cumbernauld), has a truly *national* structure that would get round the problem of separate agencies for England, Scotland and Wales. But the actual physical job of land renewal would not fall comfortably within the Land Commission's terms of reference. However, the commission could valuably assist a reclamation agency by establishing a land bank of derelict areas in advance of decisions about motorways and industrial estates – decisions which inflate the prices of even the most unholy (or holey) lands. The acquired lands could then be turned over to the national agency at the appropriate times for renewal.

During the committee debates in late 1967 and early 1968 on the Countryside Bill, Michael Jopling, M.P., supported by other Tory members, proposed that the Countryside Commission be given the job of clearing derelict land. But Mrs Eirene White, Minister of State at the Welsh Office, argued that the job required 'the full force' of the Ministry of Housing and the Welsh Office behind it.* (And so it probably does, but the government's 'full force' has been so far unimpressive.) Many of the Countryside Commission's functions would neatly co-exist with land reclamation, but on balance it is probably not strong enough and could be too easily manipulated by industry.

The national agency should however include representatives of those industries whose activities make a major and deleterious impact on the landscape. As the Countryside in 1970 organization has so ably demonstrated,† industry is much more likely to co-operate constructively if

---

* This is also the view of the Hunt Committee report of April 1969, which recommended the establishment of a derelict land reclamation agency, directed by central government, to reclaim 67,000 acres over 15 years at a total estimated cost of £100 million.

† Except in that instance, discussed earlier (p. 27), when it allowed industry not only to participate but dominate.

it participates in decisions; also, industry's needs to exploit the land must be heard and the legitimate needs satisfied.

Along with representatives of industry, planning officers from areas of high concentrations of dereliction would be part of the decision-making nucleus of a national agency. Decisions could be ratified, policies finalized, and priorities laid down by a small and well-paid board of first-class independent persons able to balance the conflicting demands on land. Decisions and actions must be delegated to whatever region tier the Clean Land Act establishes, and not centred on Whitehall, resulting in long delays and needless government involvement and interference in the details of land renewal schemes.

Indeed, the agency's headquarters should not be in Whitehall at all (though it would be ultimately responsible to the ministry there). Lancashire would be an appropriate base: the county has pioneered land renewal, it has a high concentration of dereliction (salutary for the agency's administrators to see each day) and it is situated midway on the 600-mile arc of dereliction which stretches from Cornwall through South Wales and Staffordshire, then on to the West Riding, Durham, Northumberland and the central lowlands of Scotland.

To direct its technical operations, the agency could absorb the experts on the Coal Board's opencast executive. This highly qualified team, experienced in reclamation, is in danger of dispersing altogether as coal production falls and as its members seek more promising jobs elsewhere. The agency should have under its direct authority a forestry section of seconded foresters with experience of planting on derelict land; this section could develop its own specialized nurseries. The Civic Trust and outside consultants in land-use planning and landscape architecture could be called in when required; so could plant ecologists and foresters. Universities and technical colleges should be encouraged to participate in research on land reclamation and could be brought in as advisers. In all, the agency should be no larger than absolutely necessary, with as simple and swift a decision-making structure as possible. A ministry man in Whitehall; a small independent board based in the North; a very limited number of regional councils, each with a full-time independent chief executive, part-time planning officers and representatives of industry; a highly mobile technical team, its nucleus the present opencast executive, able to move about the country when and where required. The agency would not be a dictator, but a director and co-ordinator. It would maintain liaison with the Sports Council and regional sports councils, the Nature Conservancy, preservation organizations and other bodies concerned about the landscape. The agency would be responsive to the needs of smaller local authorities and smaller industries through the members of the regional councils.

If a full-scale national land-reclamation agency along roughly these lines proves unacceptable or unattainable, at the very least a Clean Land Act should provide for a more modest agency. Both the Countryside in 1970 and the Lower Swansea Valley Project have put forward possible formats. The Countryside in 1970 has proposed that 'National and Regional Technical Advisory Groups be established under the auspices of the Ministry of Housing and Local Government, so that the necessary specialist knowledge and experience can be made available to any authority engaged in reclamation'. This advisory service 'would combine the knowledge and experience of planners, engineers, landscape architects, foresters, agriculturalists, ecologists * and others, and would include representatives of the Civic Trust, Universities and other appropriate bodies.'

The Lower Swansea Valley Project – noting that we have an Air Pollution Research Laboratory, a Water Pollution Research Laboratory, but not a Land Pollution Research Centre – recommended establishing a Land Research Unit to give 'a measure of co-ordination and direction ... which is now lacking' in land reclamation. Most of the research would be done in the universities and by industry; a Land Research Unit could ensure, among other things, 'an assembly of statistics and the preparation of a classified index of information relating to derelict land'; a review of legislation dealing with land reclamation and mineral working; research into the microbiology, ecology and chemistry of industrial wastes; research into the dispersal or treatment of wastes and the re-use of wastes.

The Money

If we are to have a real national land-reclamation agency, it will be disabled from the outset if it is not adequately

* An encouraging move in this direction is the recent formation of an Industrial Ecology Group under the auspices of the British Ecological Society. The group, which held its first meeting in May 1968, aims 'to foster interest in the ecology of environments affected by urban and industrial conditions or certain other intensive forms of human use'. Kenneth Hilton considers that this concern with environmental contamination might well justify a national agency, with executive powers and a research department, whose brief would extend beyond dealing with derelict land; it would also deal instantly with, for example, 'the kinds of problems the Torrey Canyon and Aberfan threw up'. In other words, an expert and adequately financed agency in existence at all times and equipped to act quickly and forcefully in any cases of environmental contamination.

financed. And what is absolutely essential is financial independence from the rigid constraints of the Treasury; the agency should have the powers and the financing equivalent to a nationalized industry. About £35 million * over ten years has been mentioned as sufficient to clear the hard core of existing dereliction. This is precisely the amount which the government is giving the NCB towards payments for early pensioned, redundant miners. A similar sum to rehabilitate the very environments in which most of them live would seem justified. But to be effective, the national agency would also have to prevent needless future despoliation and, whenever possible, tackle the dereliction such as that in Cornwall or Bedfordshire which is now considered intractable. And it will want, and need, to step in and assist local authorities on special projects – such as the Lower Swansea Valley – where they are neither technically nor financially capable, or where the will is lacking. There will also be administrative expenses. In all, about £5–6 million a year for the first ten years – with provision for extending the life of the clean land operation another ten years – should suffice. It would be vital that the money be guaranteed over the ten years despite freezes and squeezes that might occur.

The principle of the Ironstone Restoration Fund could, with certain additions, provide the money if extended nationally to other extractive industries. In the year ended 31 March 1967 the Ironstone Fund had a balance of nearly £550,000; in that year the ironstone owners and operators contributed nearly £115,000 and the government £40,000. If a levy per ton or cubic yard

---

* Robert Arvill has estimated £30 million and believes the restored land would be worth £10 million immediately on completion of the works.

or other suitable unit on other mineral undertakings were established and supplemented by the grants which the Exchequer now makes for land reclamation and by contributions from planning authorities in line with their abilities, the £5-6 million annual figure could be reached. The national agency could then use the income on a regional 'action area' basis: it might be that one year a large part of the money should be used along the M1 in the West Riding, another year in the South Wales valleys. Priority areas – rather like those proposed in the Plowden Report on primary schools – could be designated, and it might prove advisable to follow the Countryside in 1970's suggestion that the greater the concentration of dereliction and the number of people who would benefit from reclamation, the greater the priority. Top priority, of course, should be given to dereliction which is dangerous to life or health: spoil tips that might slide, subsided land that threatens houses, flashes or slurry ponds in which children might drown. By concentrating finances on a countrywide master plan, the most formidable expanses of dereliction – now beyond the resources and abilities and imagination of small authorities – could be tackled in a big way.

The Exchequer contributions would mean in effect a subsidy for the mineral undertakers, but the nation uses the coal, the sand and gravel and other minerals, and it is not unreasonable to expect the nation to pay towards redeeming the environment these industries disfigure. Indirectly, the present grant system subsidizes mineral operators anyway, and of course the government contributions to the Ironstone Fund directly subsidize reclamation costs. That principle extended to other mineral industries would be far preferable to the present situation: instead of the brick-makers, for example, contributing nothing towards land renewal and indeed profiting from their own dereliction, the electricity consumer or local ratepayer subsidizing their profits, under a levy system the industry would be contributing to a *national* reclamation operation.* If, indeed, the brick-makers' contention that their pits cannot be restored except at an exorbitant price proves correct, their payments could at least contribute to reclamation elsewhere. A levy of 10s. per 1,000 bricks would add only £8–10 on the cost of an ordinary house, and more than that might well be gained by bringing the derelict land back into use.

Less buoyant industries – and coal in particular – could not of course be expected to pay for all the redemption of land spoiled by their operations; the levy would need to be in line with the ability to pay. The national fund could then be used to pay the difference between what the reclamation costs and what the industry can realistically be expected to pay. However, there is no reason why the deep-mines section of the N C B could not pay something substantial by way of a levy; as Jack Lowe has noted, the N C B could pay the equivalent of what it now spends on tipping and on acquisition of land for tipping. The board would also derive the benefit from the restored land in its ownership and its bill for compensation of subsidence damage would be significantly reduced. Some planning authorities have argued that 3d. a ton on coal would suffice to restore all land currently being used for colliery tipping, as well as to afforest all derelict spoil heaps.

With a national fund, the reclamation agency could

---

* And they could afford to do so. The London Brick Company, which produces seventy per cent of all the fletton bricks in the nation, had before-tax profits in 1967 of more than £4 million, and more than £3 million in 1966 – a poor year for the construction industry.

examine those proposals for transporting heaps into holes, where the economics of transport have so far prevented action. In Lancashire, Aylmer Coates has been pressing for years for the reclamation of a vast subsided wasteland at Hey Brook (subsided on average by twenty-three feet) with spoil from Parkside Colliery a few miles away, but the scheme has got nowhere because of a difference of a few shillings per ton between the county council's and the Coal Board's estimates of what the operation would cost. In Cornwall, H. W. J. Heck says that only 2s. or 3s. a ton separates the amount British Rail would need to charge to convey china-clay waste from St Austell to London and the amount that would be a paying proposition for the china-clay extractors. Scrutiny of the Nottingham-shire–Bedfordshire transport proposal might reveal that the ultimate benefits would be sufficient to use the fund for subsidizing the operation. Lord Robens has said:

> It may sometimes pay us handsomely to subsidize the trans-port of waste material if the cost of placing it where it is needed or where it will do the least harm to environment is more than industry can bear. This might often be cheaper than subsidizing the ultimate cost of reclaiming one, or possibly two, areas of despoiled land.

The agency could also investigate the economics of back stowage of spoil in deep mines – filling the cavities with the waste. This is done at very few pits in Britain (although John Oxenham has noted that it is common practice on the Continent) and the N C B claims that it is far too expensive * and technically difficult. The board

---

* The N C B finds it cheaper to pay compensation for damage from subsidence – required under a 1957 Act – than to pay for back stow-age. In any event, the N C B's cries of poverty may not stand up in future years. The board has made a small profit in the past two years,

claims that it has done the arithmetic, but it refuses to disclose the figures. If the figures were made public, it would be possible to consider whether a subsidy in the interests of environmental improvement would be feasible. A national agency could do this.

As for the technical difficulties of back stowing, Garth Christian has probably provided the answer: 'Once responsibility for restoring land is placed firmly on the shoulders of the extractors, means are usually devised to enable the land to be restored at a reasonable price.' Sylvia Crowe has made the same point, adding: 'It is only when the land is regarded as expendable that devastation continues.' That is precisely what happened with ironstone; under pressure, the machinery was evolved, the technical difficulties overcome, to restore the land. This could happen with back stowage in deep mines.*

Geoffrey Rippon, M.P., the Opposition spokesman on housing and local government, says, 'I do think that the economic benefits of land rehabilitation tend not to be highlighted sufficiently. The very high price of building land and the importance of domestic agriculture from the point of view of import saving both guarantee the community an excellent return on grants for the rehabilitation of land.' J. M. van Staveren, director of the International Institute for Land Reclamation and Improvement, in

---

and in May 1968 it announced that it was entering the computer service business and expected to earn from that up to £15 million a year within the next three to four years. The board also confirmed that it had made a big North Sea gas strike in a field it owns jointly with an American oil company. A slimmed-down, modernized Coal Board may well be able to pay its fair share towards land reclamation.

* In February 1968 *Colliery Engineering* reported a new method of hydraulic stowing, using a chemical reagent mixed with slurry, which reduces operating costs by thirty per cent.

Wageningen, Netherlands, admits that from the view of either private enterprise or government, reclaimed land may not appear directly to pay for itself. But he cites 'all kinds of indirect effects which yield positive values', including extension of employment, secondary industries based on the primary ones, saving on food imports, amelioration of traffic problems, wider facilities for recreation and 'a contribution to sound social development'.

A series of really thorough cost-benefit analyses (drawing in university departments) could be one of the agency's most valuable if formidable tasks. What is the cost in the long run of continuing to dump coal spoil on the surface rather than stow it underground? Is the plonking of housing or an industrial estate on reclaimed land to bring an immediate profit, the right thing to do in the long term? Might not an immediately unprofitable use of land for recreation pay eventually? Might not surplus power station ash be considered a national asset for grand-scale land reclamation, resulting in long-range social benefits that merit underwriting its transport by rail or pipeline? * In areas of concentrated dereliction, is it in the region's interest to exploit the usable shale in spoil tips for as long as possible, or does the very presence of those tips over long periods outweigh the economic benefits by spreading social malaise and discouraging new industry? Incineration of town refuse is cheaper for a local authority than controlled tipping – but from a

* H. E. Bracey has noted that in past years nearly half the annual production of fuel ash has been dumped at sea. This probably made sense to the C E G B, but from the standpoint of the national interest it was an absurd waste of valuable land-filling material. Today the C E G B says, 'With the increasing use and value of ash, the amount dumped at sea has been drastically reduced and two large stations previously using this method have been converted to allow commercial sales.'

regional or national point of view, might it not pay to combine pulverized refuse with inert materials like colliery waste and so reclaim large pits and marshlands?* In Japan about eight million tons of blast furnace slag is used each year for land reclamation; in Britain nearly all slag is sold for industrial uses; in the long term would it pay us to divert to land renewal some of the ten million tons of slag we produce? These are the kind of questions that cost-benefit studies by a national land agency might answer.

The Objectives

The overall objectives of the proposed Clean Land Act, national agency and operating fund would of course be to clear yesterday's dereliction, control today's and prevent tomorrow's. Whenever possible, minerals extraction should be made *constructive*, a vehicle for the rehabilitation of dereliction. New and exciting land contours can often be created from spoil tips. Degraded landscapes near urban areas can sometimes be turned into 'blue belts', chains of lakes devised by constructive exploitation of gravel.† In one sense, derelict land (like war-damaged land) is a positive asset, because its revival offers such creative possibilities. In the West Riding, John Casson speaks of his 'lovely cushion of dereliction ... they don't have our *advantage* in the South'.

* In Liverpool, controlled tipping of town refuse has formed the foundations of 300 acres of playing fields, and Liverpool Promenade is literally built on rubbish.

† This is happening at Colwick in Nottinghamshire, where the county planners and Hoveringham Gravels have agreed on a fourteen-year extraction programme. during which the recreational afteruse is governing the way the firm digs for gravel. By 1980, there will be two large 'purpose-built' lakes covering 110 acres.

To turn landscape destruction into constructive after-uses means co-ordinating the building of roads and motorways with the reclamation of derelict land. In some cases the line of major roads might be adjusted to absorb dereliction. In any case, the topsoil removed for road-building must not be wasted but used on any nearby dereliction. The Ministry of Transport's contracts for roads should not stop at the roads themselves, but consider any useful reclamation that could be done along the route at the same time as the road-building and with the same machinery.

Industries which produce unmanageable heaps can sometimes be sited near industries which produce hopeless holes – e.g. power stations and gravel workings, the fuel ash piped straight into the pits. Co-ordinating tipping and filling (using computers to co-ordinate operations) is cheaper and reclaims two areas of land in one operation. J. R. Caseley of the Institution of Civil Engineers has said, 'It is essential that all possible development interests in a given region should be brought together in order to ensure that haulage distances are kept to a minimum.' And, as John Oxenham has argued, 'It is also essential that the after-use of restoration be known in advance, so as to merge extraction and redemption in one continuous process.' Much restoration can be carried out *progressively*, as parts of clay or gravel pits are worked out, rather than leaving all redemption until the whole working area is exhausted. Where this is impossible, interim landscaping could be required, especially at long-life workings which create a noise nuisance, dust and ugliness for many years.

A national reclamation agency could also examine whether it might be possible to end the General Development Order which permits the Coal Board to continue sterilizing hundreds of acres a year with spoil tips. Some compensation system might have to be worked out – although at post-1948 workings, where the NCB is required to comply with reasonable restoration conditions imposed by planning authorities, the board appears to have no major difficulties in complying. 'It is indefensible that the freedom of tipping without control should continue for so long,' says Jack Lowe. And the Civic Trust has noted one of the most serious effects of the General Development Order: 'There is no obligation on the NCB to integrate its own planning with the planning authority's wider objectives.'

The reclamation agency must see that reasonable but firm planning controls are imposed on industry to restore its lands, – or at least to landscape – and so curb tomorrow's dereliction at its source. In Durham, Richard Atkinson says:

We have for some years been applying a 'landscape condition' to planning consents ... this requires the submission and approval of a proper landscape scheme. Getting an adequate scheme in the face of ignorance and often unwillingness on the part of the applicant is often difficult. Seeing that it is carried out is even more difficult.

An industry's past performance on land reclamation might well guide the planning permissions. The conditions must not be petty or frustrating, but unambiguous and fair. Once imposed, they must be fulfilled. As Shropshire's planner, N. Bennett, argues: 'I think it is essential that no further dereliction of land should be allowed to take place, that planning conditions on mineral workings should be stringent and seen to be enforced. And once restoration is accomplished, there must be careful after-management, to see that the grass and trees thrive and that the renewed land does not slide back into dereliction.'

All possible uses for waste in heaps should be further explored. Shale can be used in the manufacture of compost fertilizer. Duff coal has been burnt by power stations. The Road Research Laboratory has found that burnt colliery shale and spent oil shale are satisfactory for road fills and sub-bases; the addition of a small proportion of cement is required to ensure its suitability under freezing conditions. Quarry waste can be used in bricks, concrete tiles and precasting building units. Ash and clinker can be used in breeze blocks, lightweight walling, and as an aggregate for lightweight concrete or as a cement diluent. The wastes in Scotland's oil shale bings can be used, mixed with lime, in brick-making. Crushed concrete from abandoned airfields can be used in road sub-bases. The Coal Board says it is working on 'complete processing of pit waste at its source, thereby eliminating all tipping'; the wastes may one day be made at the pit head into lightweight building blocks for the precast building industry. The National Research Development Corporation is providing backing for a Wolverhampton firm's new process for making fertilizer (called 'Sweetsoil') from household waste. The slag industry is a model of what can be done with wastes when all the possible uses are really explored.

More study is needed on piping power station ash in slurry form into pits. Two miles or so is the usual distance now; with technological improvements and a subsidy, greater distances might well prove feasible. Offshore gravel digging could be further explored, to avoid pockmarking the land to such an extent. Professor M. J. Lighthill has said:

Already over ten per cent of sand and gravel is dredged

from the sea bed and that is one resource of the continental shelf that needs to be more fully exploited, provided really careful scientific analyses are made to identify where dredging can be done without danger to fisheries or to coastal erosion.

Derelict land can often be turned to recreation, and we need to explore further the possibilities of making recreation pay and so giving an economic return on reclaimed lands. There should not be fees everywhere, but people are clearly prepared to pay for leisure pursuits that give them good value for money. As one county planner puts it: 'The stately home boys have been on to that a long time ago.' (More than 18 million people visited historic houses in 1967.) John Casson and L. A. King have noted that more and more people are diverting the maximum of their surplus money to recreation – touring holidays, caravans, boats: 'This new economic force and the desire for recreational opportunity might now make possible the attainment of the objectives of conserving and cleaning up the countryside which had begun to seem unattainable.'

According to the British Travel Association, more than thirty million holidays were taken inside Britain in 1967; holidaymakers spent £560 million. The association's *Pilot National Recreation Survey* in conjunction with the University of Keele, found a tremendous growth in the popularity of golf, fishing and inland boating and sailing – all activities for which people are prepared to pay * and for which reclaimed colliery lands or reshaped and planted refuse dumps or gravel pits near urban areas could be suitable. Near Reading a gravel operator is spending about £6 million to create a great recreation area from worked-out pits; the firm expects the project to

* *The Times* has pointed out that sailing clubs are quite prepared to pay up to £25 an acre annual rental for the joys of wet gravel pits.

pay handsomely. This kind of 'profiteering' from holes in the ground is desirable. The 1962 report, *Outdoor Recreation for America*, said: 'Outdoor recreation brings about economic as well as social benefits – the millions and millions of people seeking the outdoors generated an estimated $20 billion a year market for goods and services.' The commission which produced the report included representatives of mining industries as well as recreation and conservation groups. In Britain too we need to harness imaginatively the extractive industries and land reclamation to the fast growing demands for leisure facilities.

The Will

We need a radical change in attitudes about dereliction. The Lower Swansea Valley Project has shown how people can be brought together in the attack on one city's shame – *if* the will is there. The will behind the Swansea project should be repeated on a thousand other ravaged landscapes.

If we fail to develop the will, our environment will continue to deteriorate, our contempt for environment will be proved. We shall be an economically prosperous people living in a physically impoverished land. Sylvia Crowe has written: 'It is time to abandon the mentality of the nomadic tribes who take all they can from the land and pass on, and to learn instead to recreate the landscape in which we have to live.'

Stewart Udall has warned: 'We are no more than brief tenants of this planet. By exercise of choice, or by careless default, we shape the land legacy of our descendants.' Udall spoke of America; what he said applies even more to our small and crowded island.

Derelict Britain

Our grandfathers tore wealth from this land, willing us a prosperity devalued by dereliction. Are we to do the same for our grandchildren? If we do they will curse us and they will be right to do so.

A Note on Main Sources

General

Three booklets are concerned entirely with dereliction. The Ministry of Housing and Local Government's *New Life for Dead Lands* (H M S O, 1963), although unrealistically cheery and drastically undercritical of its own role, is a clear exposition of the problem – at the time. The Civic Trust's *Derelict Land* (1964; 3rd impression, 1967) is more thorough and more detached from the official view; it is, however, rather muted, and government and industry are treated too meekly. More outspoken is the report of Study Group 12, *Reclamation and Clearance of Derelict Land*, at the second Countryside in 1970 conference (Royal Society of Arts and Nature Conservancy, 1965). This pamphlet offers sensible and sometimes bold recommendations for action.

Four books about planning and environment include competent discussions of dereliction. The most recent and valuable is *Man and Environment* (Penguin Books, 1967) by Robert Arvill.* He discusses derelict land in the broad context of the world twentieth-century man is creating – and destroying. In *Tomorrow's Countryside: the Road to the Seventies* (John Murray, 1966) the late Garth Christian devoted a thoughtful and well-argued chapter to 'Redeeming Man's Mistakes'. A brief and clear discussion of land reclamation as part of overall planning policies can be found in J. B. Cullingworth's *Town and Country Planning in England and Wales* (George Allen

---

* The pen-name of one of the country's leading nature conservationists.

& Unwin, 1967). This is a revised edition of a 1964 book, yet disappointingly relies on government statistics of dereliction that are thirteen years old. The disgrace of industrial dereliction is underlined at many points in *Tomorrow's Landscape* (Architectural Press, 1956; 2nd impression, 1963) by Sylvia Crowe, a prominent landscape architect with a sharp eye for man-made blight and the knack of presenting constructive cures.

Technical

While *Reclaiming Derelict Land* (Faber & Faber, 1966) by John Oxenham surveys the subject broadly, it is particularly valuable for the technical details of how to do the job of land renewal. It should be a required handbook for all planning officers and voluntary groups concerned with cleansing the landscape. *Ecology and the Industrial Society*, edited by G. T. Goodman (Blackwell Scientific Publications, Oxford, 1965), is a collection of technical papers on the whole range of problems arising from man's pollution of his environment. It includes authoritative papers, presented at a British Ecological Society symposium, on world-wide efforts to reclaim industrial wastelands and on revegetation of land spoiled by industry.

Area Studies

By far the most detailed and constructive study of dereliction in a defined area is *The Lower Swansea Valley Project** (Longmans, 1967), edited by the project's director, K. J. Hilton. It summarizes in layman's language the

---

* My Chapters 5 and 6 are based almost wholly on this book; Chapters 4 and 7 are based partly on it.

results of the five-year study and advances imaginative proposals for restoration that would have application to many other despoiled areas in the country. Readers desiring the whole remarkable story of the project are advised to read this book.

The project produced twelve study reports, which would interest the specialist in the problems of derelict land. Sets of the reports have been deposited at the University College of Swansea library, the National Library of Wales in Aberystwyth, the Guildhall in Swansea and the British Museum. The reports are as follows:

1. The Human Ecology of the Lower Swansea Valley. (Margaret Stacey)
2. Report on Transportation and Physical Planning in the Lower Swansea Valley. (R. D. Worrall)
3. Report on the Hydrology of the Lower Swansea Valley. (D. C. Ledger)
4. Report on the Geology of the Lower Swansea Valley. (W. F. G. Cardy)
5. The Soil Mechanics and Foundation Engineering Survey of the Lower Swansea Valley Project Area. (H. G. Clapham, H. E. Evans, and F. E. Weare)
6. The Prospects for Industrial Use of the Lower Swansea Valley – A Study of Land Use in a Regional Context. (Susanne H. Spence)
7. Lower Swansea Valley: Housing Report. (Margaret Stacey)
8. Lower Swansea Valley: Open Space Report. (Margaret Stacey)
9. Plant Ecology of the Lower Swansea Valley:
   (a) Vegetation Trials. (Ruth L. Gadgil)
   (b) Large-scale Grass Trials. (L. J. Hooper and R. Garret Jones)
   (c) Soils. (E. M. Bridges.)

10. Soil Biology of the Lower Swansea Valley. (P. D. Gadgil)

11. Afforestation of the Lower Swansea Valley. (B. R. G. Holt)

12. Tips and Tip Working in the Lower Swansea Valley. (G. Holt)

13. Estimation of Quantities of Materials in the Northern Part of the Lower Swansea Valley Project Area. (H. E. Evans)

14. Report on a Preliminary Investigation to Determine the Feasibility of Creating an Artificial Lake in the Lower Swansea Valley Project Area. (R. E. Davies)

Among other useful studies of regional or sub-regional dereliction is *Bedfordshire Brickfield: a planning appraisal of the problems of the fletton brick manufacturing area in Bedfordshire* (Bedfordshire County Council, 1967). The county's planning officer, Geoffrey Cowley, argues for a solution to the brickfield dereliction. A no-nonsense analysis of another area can be found in *Derelict Land in the North East* (Durham County Council, 1965). This booklet outlines clearly the obstacles preventing 'a satisfactory rate of reclamation'.

Journals and Articles

Derelict land and land reclamation are dealt with quite frequently in the *Journal of the Town Planning Institute*. Particularly valuable discussions include 'The Industrial Landscape' by J. R. Atkinson (April 1963) and 'The Lower Swansea Valley Project' by K. J. Hilton (March 1965). Useful articles have appeared in *Town and Country Planning*, including 'Planned Dereliction!' by H. J. Lowe (February 1967) and 'The Lower Swansea Valley Project' by D. F. Banwell (November 1967). *Town Plan-*

ning Review has published 'The Treatment of Waste Slate Heaps' by C. T. Crompton (January 1967) and 'Derelict Land in South Wales' by Trevor M. Thomas (July 1966).

Other discussions of land reclamation include 'Landscape Reclamation Research Project: University of Newcastle upon Tyne' by M. F. Downing and C. J. Vyle in the *Journal of the Institute of Landscape Architects* (August 1966); 'The 1967 Sub-Committee Survey of the Nature of the Technical Advice Required When Treating Land Affected by Industry,' G. T. Goodman (ed.), in the *Journal of Ecology* 55; 'Industry and the Use of Land' by Lord Robens, in *Estates Gazette*, 8 May 1965; and 'Landscaping Planning Approach to Land Reclamation' by C. J. Vyle, in *Park Administration*, January/February 1968.

Index

Abercrombie, Sir Patrick, 182
Aberfan, 11–12, 40, 44, 56, 155
Agricultural chemicals, 16n.
Agriculture, Ministry of, 16n., 24n.,
    71n., 165, 192, 209
Airfields, 52, 177
Airports, 18–19
Allison, John, 132, 142–3, 148
Amble, 184
Appalachians, 199
Arvill, Robert, 146, 214n., 227
Associated Portland Cement
    Manufacturers, 26, 200
Atkinson, James, 133
Atkinson, Richard, 23, 26, 28–9,
    34–5, 173, 181, 222, 230
Atom, 202
Atomic energy, 202–3
Atherton, 176

Bacton, 201
Bainbridge, G. R., 202
Baker, F. C., 171
Ban-forests, 56
Banwell, D. F., 142, 146, 149–50,
    153–4, 230
Beaver, S. H., 71
Bedford Corporation, 190
Bedfordshire, 39, 48–9, 188–92
Bedfordshire Brickfield, 188–92, 230
Beeching, Lord, 53
Bell, George, 88
Bennett, N., 186, 222
Best, Robin, 16n., 73
Bickerstaffe Colliery, 160
Birds (Swansea), 134n.
Birmingham University, 71
Blackman, G. A. W., 170
Board of Trade, *see* Trade, Board of
Bon-y-Maen, 95, 105

Boote, Robert, 37, 130
Borrow, George, 83
Bracey, H. E., 219n.
Branston, 177n.
Brewer, F. E., 176
Brick-clay dereliction, 29, 167–70,
    188–92
Bridges, Robert, 159
Bristow, J. P., 188–91
Britain and the Beast, 79
British Association for the
    Advancement of Science, 34
British Ecological Society, 33, 71,
    213n., 228
British Rail, 52–4, 105, 168, 187,
    191–2, 196n., 217
British Sugar Corporation, 168n.
British Transport Docks Board, 148
British Travel Association, 224
British Waterways Board, 54
Bryn Hall, 161–2
Burtonwood Air Base, 186

Calder Hall, 202–3
Camborne, 174
Campbell, Ian, 163n.
Cannock reclamation plan, 185
Carnon Valley, 174
Caseley, J. R., 221
Casson, John, 34, 68, 173, 193, 220,
    224
Castle Eden Dene, 178
Central Council of Physical
    Recreation, 18
Central Electricity Generating
    Board, 29, 167–70, 219n.
Cheshire, 41–2
China-clay dereliction, 187–8
Christian, Garth, 52n., 107n., 218,
    227

Index

Civic Amenities Act, 117n.
Civic Trust
  definition of reclamation, 15n.
  Derelict Land, 25, 74, 222
  dereliction, costs of, 30, 204
  dereliction, statistics, 15, 200
  Eyesores, 22
  Lee Valley plan, 49, 181-4
  Operation Springclean, 177-8
  Rhondda Valleys plan, 178-9, 194
  role in reclamation, 209, 211, 213
  tree transplanting, 70
  Youth Enterprise, 178
Clean Air Act, 73n.
Clean Air Conference, 202
'Clean Land Act', 36, 206-8,
    211-12, 220
Cleworth Colliery, 12
Cliffe, Charles Frederick, 83-4
Coal Board, *see* National Coal Board
Coalbrookdale, 186
Coates, Aylmer, 30, 69, 75, 162, 217
Cockenzie power station, 186
Coldrife opencast mine, 185
Colliery Engineering, 218
Cologne, 197
Colwick, 220n.
Commons, Open Spaces and Foot-
    paths Preservation Society,
    163n.
Community Service Volunteers,
    178-9
Coppock, J. T., 16n.
Corby New Town, 186
Cordle, John, 47n.
Cornwall, 42, 49, 174, 187-8, 217
Cossall Colliery, 172
Costs of Economic Growth, 21-2
Council for Nature, 56
Council for the Preservation of
    Rural England, 45-6
Council for the Protection of Rural
    Wales, 45
Country parks, 58
Countryside Act, 58, 154, 210

Countryside Commission, 210
Countryside in 1970 Committee
  study group, dereliction, 30, 38-9,
      61, 66, 69, 205, 210-12
  study group, technolgy in
      conservation, 46
  sub-group, industry and
      countryside, 27-8
Cowley, Geoffrey, 188, 192, 230
Crompton, C. T., 46n., 231
Crowe, Sylvia, 106, 218, 225, 228
Cullingworth, J. B., 227
Cumberland, 42, 176, 203
Cwmbran New Town, 152

Dartington Research Trust, 177
Dartmoor, 51
Defence, Ministry of, 50-52, 177
Defoe, Daniel, 80-81
Derbyshire, 69
Derelict Land, 25, 74, 227
Distribution of Industry Act, 89
Dower, Michael, 17, 177
Downing, M. F., 231
Drake, James, 193n.
Druridge Bay, 184
Durham, County
  dereliction, 28, 42, 48, 192-3, 230
  reclamation, 61, 76, 171, 173-4,
      222
Dutch State Mines, 197

Easington, 201
East Anglia Economic Planning
    Council, 53
East Lothian County Council, 186
East Midlands Economic Planning
    Council, 35-6
Ebbw Vale, 86
Ecology and the Industrial Society, 228
Economic Affairs, Department of,
    67
Edinburgh, Duke of, 154, 156
Edinburgh University, 71n.
Electricity Act, 167

Index

Enfield, 183
English Journey, 48
Essex, 183
Estates Gazette, 231
Evans, Gwynfor, 11, 44
Eyesores, 22

Fforestfach industrial estate, 89, 118, 152
Fife, 175
Firestone Tyre and Rubber Co., 122n.
Flintoff, Frank, 57
Forestry Commission, 56, 65–6, 71n., 96, 106, 154–5
Forth Road Bridge, 174

Gadgil, P. D., 113
Gas Council, 201–2
Gedling Colliery, 12
General Development Order, 28, 40, 67, 173, 221–2
George Cohen Sons and Co., 133
German Railways, 196n.
Germany, 194–7
Gibson-Watt, David, 53
Gillie, F. Blaise, 143n.
Glamorgan, 42
Glamorgan County Council, 147
Goodman, Gordon, 145, 228, 231
Graham, Michael, 70, 176
Grangemouth, 175
Grants for reclamation, *see* Reclamation
Greater London Council, 57, 183, 190n., 191
Greater London Plan, 182
Greenwood, Anthony, 23, 63
Gregory, Malcolm, 164, 167
Griffith, H., 82–3
Gulbenkian Foundation, 176

Hackney, 182
Hamburg, 197

Harris, Christopher, 94, 135–6n., 137n.
Hawkes, Jacquetta, 38
Heck, H. W. J., 174, 187–8, 217
Herald of Wales, 85, 90
Hertfordshire, 182–3
Hey Brook, 217
Hilton, Kenneth, 94, 109, 130, 143n., 155, 195–7, 213n., 228, 230
Housing, 18
Housing and Local Government, Ministry of
   advice on reclamation, 24, 171, 174, 209
   definition of dereliction, 38–40
   dereliction, statistics, 40–44
   grants for reclamation, 23, 64–5, 68, 209
   New Life for Dead Lands, 20, 35, 227
   planning conditions, 29, 44, 67–8, 72
   reclamation, statistics, 40–44
Hoveringham Gravels, 220n.
Howarth, Robert, 32
Hunt Committee, 35
Hydraulic seeding, 70–71

Imber, 51
Imperial Smelting Corporation, 133–4
Ince-in-Makerfield, 42, 44
Industrial Development Act, 62
Inland Waterways Association, 179
Institution of Civil Engineers, 221
International Institute for Land Reclamation and Improvement, 218–19
International Voluntary Service, 107, 117, 144n., 179
Ironstone reclamation, 164–7
Ironstone Reclamation Fund, 47, 165, 207, 214–15

Index

Jenkin, David, 81–2
Johnson, Lyndon, 198
Jones, Robin Huws, 92, 95, 143n.
Jopling, Michael, 210
Joseph, Sir Keith, 20
Journal of Ecology, 231
*Journal of the Institute of Landscape
  Architects*, 231
*Journal of the Town Planning
  Institute*, 230

Keele University, 224
Kew Gardens, 68n.
Kidwelly, 95
Kilvey Hill, 121, 149
King, L. A., 34, 224
Kirby-in-Ashfield, 172
Knabe, Wilhelm, 197

Lancashire
  Community Council of, 176
  derelicton, 12, 42, 74–5, 160–64,
    217
  land costs, 69
  local authority structure, 66–7
  motorways, 193n.
  reclamation, 61, 76, 98, 160–64,
    176, 186
Land and Natural Resources,
  Ministry of, 209
Land Commission, 209–10
Land reclamation, *see* Reclamation
Land Use Consultants, 184–5
Landore, 79n., 93, 95, 105, 148, 153
Landore Colliery, 82
Lane, John, 81
Latham, A., 69
Lawrence, D. H., 50
Lee Valley plan, 49, 181–4
Lee Valley Regional Park Act, 182
Lee Valley Regional Park
  Authority, 183
Leeds University, 71
Leicestershire, 164
Leisure, *see* Recreation

Leisure in the Countryside, 58
Lighthill, M. J., 223–4
Limburg, 197
Lincolnshire, 42, 164
Litter Act, 117
Liverpool, 220n.
Livingstone New Town, 175
Llanelli, 114
Llansamlet, 94, 100, 135n.
Llansamlet Copper and Arsenic
  Works, 105
Local Authorities (Land) Act, 63n.
Local Employment Act, 90
Local Government Act, 63
Local Government Commission, 147
Local Government in Wales, 66
Local government, Royal
  Commissions, 66
Lochgelly, 175
Lochore Meadows, 175
London Brick Company, 178n.,
  188–91
Long Lane Colliery, 162
Lothians, 76
Lothians Regional Survey, 48
Lowe, Jack, 14, 19, 73–4, 172, 216,
  222, 230
Lower Swansea Valley, *see* Swansea
Lulworth, 51

MacDermot, Niall, 192
Man and Environment, 146, 227
Manning, J. C., 85
Manselton, 95
Mather, T., 162
Mather, William, 75
McBride, N., 132
McDermott, M., 113–14
Merionethshire, 175
Midlothian and West Lothian Joint
  Planning Advisory Committee,
  185–6
Mineral Workings Act, 165, 207
Mishan, E. J., 21–2
Mitchell Main Colliery, 172

Monmouthshire Canal, 58
Morgan, D. A., 133–4
Morgan, E. Victor, 125
Moorhouse, Geoffrey, 74
Morris, Sir John, 82
Morris, Percy, 143n.
Morriston, 82, 94, 135–6n.
Mumford, Lewis, 160

Nairn, Ian, 25–6, 47, 162
National Agricultural Advisory
    Service, 71, 98, 106
National Coal Board
    Aberfan, 11–12
    land-moving machinery, 70
    land use, 44–5, 69, 73n., 192,
        196, 216–18, 221–2
    opencast reclamation, 170–73,
        184–5
    production, 203–4, 223
    surveys of dereliction, 48
    tree-transplanting, 70, 178
National Parks and Access to the
    Countryside Act, 63
National Playing Fields Association,
    18
National Research Development
    Corporation, 223
National Trust, 179
Natural Environment Research
    Council, 145
Natural gas, 201–2
Nature Conservancy, 37, 71n., 130,
    212
Netherlands, 197–8, 218–19
New Life for Dead Lands, 20, 35–6,
    227
New Society, 102–3n., 155
Newcastle, 174, 184
Newcastle University, 57, 71n., 174,
    231
Newport, 86
Newton, D. E., 52
Norfolk, 53
Norfolk Broads, 185

North East planning officers, 35–6
North Makerfield, 160
North Riding, 41
North West, The, 67
North West Economic Planning
    Council, 22, 74–5, 177–8
Northamptonshire, 164–7, 186
Northern Economic Planning
    Council, 63
Northern Ireland, 40n.
Northumberland
    dereliction, 42, 48
    reclamation, 42, 171–2, 174, 184
Nottinghamshire
    dereliction, 12, 40, 50, 74
    reclamation, 172, 177, 191–2,
        220n.
Nuffield Foundation, 94

Oliver, J., 113
Opencast Executive, 170–72, 211
Operation Springclean, 177–8
Orwell, George, 47, 91
Other England, The, 74
Outdoor Recreation for America, 225
Oxenham, John, 31, 36, 46, 57, 60,
    70, 217, 221, 228
Oxfordshire, 164

Park Administration, 231
Parkside Colliery, 217
Parry, John, 93–4, 143n.
Peak Forest Canal, 179
Pentrechwych, 95
Perry, Norman, 195–6
Peterborough reclamation project,
    29, 167–70
Picketts Lock, 183
Pilot National Recreation Survey, 224
Polesworth reclamation project, 185
Port Talbot, 86
Porth, 194
Potter, Dennis, 11, 155
Pounds, Norman, 195–6

Index

Power, Ministry of, 209
Priestley, J. B., 48
Public Building and Works,
    Ministry of, 209
Public Health Inspectors,
    Association of, 33, 201
Pulverized fuel ash, 167–70

Quakers, 176

Ramblers' Association, 58
Reclaiming Derelict Land, 31, 70, 228
Reclamation
    costs, 31–2, 61
    grants, 22–3, 61–5, 68
*Reclamation and Clearance of Derelict
    Land*, 227
Recreation, 17–18, 55–6, 58
Reese Committee, 73
Refuse, 57, 190, 219–20
Rhondda Valleys, 178–9, 194
Rhondda Youth Action, 178–9
Richard Thomas and Baldwin,
    134n.
Riley, D. W., 28
Rippon, Geoffrey, 218
Risley Royal Ordnance Factory, 186
Rivers (Protection of Pollution)
    Act, 121
Road Research Laboratory, 223
Roads, 17
Robens, Lord, 13–14, 44–5, 70,
    178n., 195, 202, 217, 231
Robinson, Kenneth, 209
Rochdale, 75
Rosser, Colin, 94, 135–6n., 137n.
Royal Society for the Prevention of
    Accidents, 33
Ruhr, 194–7
Ruhr Planning Authority, 194–7,
    208
Rutland, 164

St Austell, 49, 187, 217

Sand and gravel, 200–201, 223–4
Sand and Gravel Association of
    Great Britain, 45
Sandys, Duncan, 117n.
Schumacher, F. E., 202
Science Research Council, 93
Scott, Peter, 58
Scottish Development Department,
    40, 185–6
Sculthorpe, 177n.
Senior, Derek, 74, 206n.
Sharp, Thomas, 32
Sherpherd, Malcolm, 178
Shropshire, 186, 222
Slagheaps Bill, 47n., 207
Smith, T. Dan, 63, 65, 68
Soil-making, 71
South Africa, 198
South East Economic Planning
    Council, 45
South East regional sports councils,
    58
South of Scotland Electricity Board,
    186
South Stratford Canal, 179
South Wales Evening Post, 93–4, 109,
    131, 135, 145
Southall, R. B., 143n.
Special Areas Act, 89
Sports Council, 183, 212
Stacey, Margaret, 81n., 102–3n.,
    134–5, 137–8, 147, 150–51
Staffordshire, 42, 173, 185
Stamp, Sir Dudley, 17, 19
Stephenson, John, 33, 57
Stewart, Sir Ronald, 191n.
Stewart and Lloyd, 166
Stewartby Lake, 190
Stoke-on-Trent, 72
Stourbridge Canal, 179
Swansea
    history, 80–85
    town centre, 79–80, 90
    University College of, 24, 92–6,
        136

Index

Lower Swansea Valley
  dereliction, 49, 79, 83–91, 92,
    104–5
  history of industry, 79, 81–9
  land ownership, 69
  reclamation proposals, 88–91
  recreation, 55–6
  Tawe River, 81–3, 95
  waterways, 54, 88
Lower Swansea Valley Project,
    109–10, 228–9
Lower Swansea Valley Project
  administrative machinery,
    123–5
  air pollution surveys, 99–100,
    113–14
  area of project, 94–5
  blueprint, 24, 76, 109–10
  botanical surveys, 71, 84, 98,
    111–12
  Civic Trust participation, 117
  climatological surveys, 99, 113
  conclusions, 110–18
  cost-benefit analysis, 30, 125–9
  evaluation of project, 138–43
  Forestry Commission
    participation, 96, 106, 154–5
  geological surveys, 96–7,
    110–11
  housing surveys, 103–4, 114–16,
    120–21
  human ecology surveys, 102–3,
    114–16, 138
  hydrological surveys, 98–9,
    112–13
  industry and employment in
    valley, 95, 101–2, 116–17,
    118–20, 152–3
  industry participation, 132–4
  Land Research Unit, 213
  land-use plan, 118–23
  National Agricultural Advisory
    Service participation, 98, 106
  Nuffield Foundation
    participation, 94
  open-space proposals, 116,
    119–23, 141, 154–5
  organization of project, 96
  physical studies, 96–102, 110–14
  reclamation, 104–5, 144–5
  recommendations, 110–18 (*see
    also* land-use plan)
  socio-economic studies, 100–4
  South-West Wales subregion,
    101–2, 116–19
  Swansea Corporation
    participation, 93, 96, 117,
    131–2, 136–8, 146–8, 151
  terms of reference, 92
  transportation surveys, 100–101,
    114
  vegetation trials, 98, 105–8,
    111–12, 144–5
  waste disposal in valley, 95,
    117
  waterways, 98–9, 112–13, 121–3
  Welsh Office participation, 93,
    96, 124, 132, 146–9, 151

Taylor, John, 26–7, 200
Taylor, Maurice, 175
Telford New Town, 186
Tennessee Valley Authority, 143
Territorial Army, 96, 105
Testament of Beauty, The, 159
Thomas, Trevor, 47, 231
Three Sisters tips, 162
Times, The, 224n.
Tomorrow's Countryside, 227
Tomorrow's Landscape, 227
Tottenham Lock, 182
Town and Country Planning, 142n., 230
Town and Country Planning Act
    1947, 165
Town and Country Planning Act
    1968, 151
*Town and Country Planning in England
    and Wales*, 227
Town Planning Review, 230–31

Index

Trade, Board of, 62–4, 148–9, 151, 209

Transport, Ministry of, 54–5, 208–9, 221

Tyler, G. Froom, 131

Tyneham, 51

Udall, Stewart, 199, 225

United Kingdom Atomic Energy Authority, 203

United States, 194, 198–9

Vale, Edmund, 79

Van Staveren, J. M., 218–19

Voluntary reclamation efforts, 176–80

Vyle, C. J., 195, 197, 231

Wallace, Lew, 161

Wallbrook, 173

Walton, Izaak, 181

Ward, W. J., 132, 148, 150, 152–3

Ware, 182

Warrington, 186

Waterways, 54–5

Watkins, Iorwerth, 131, 145–7, 149, 155

Wear River, 178

Welsh Office, 11, 62, 64, 175–6, 194, 208

West Ham, 182

West Ham College of Technology, 183

West Lothian, 175

West Midlands, 59

West Midlands Sports Council, 185

West Riding
  dereliction, 34, 42, 48, 53, 193, 220
  reclamation, 76, 172–3, 176

West Wales River Authority, 134

Western Mail, 62n.

Westfield, 175

Wey River, 179

Whalley's Basin, 161

White, Eirene, 210

White Rock Copper, Lead and Silver Works, 105n., 149

Wibberley, Gerald, 15–16

Williams, A., 132

Windscale, 203

Witwatersrand goldfield, 198

Woodlands, 56

York University, 71n.

Yorkshire and Humberside Economic Planning Council, 3?

Yorkshire and Humberside region, 178, 208

Yorkshire Imperial Metals, 132–3

Young, Hugo, 55

Youth Enterprise, 178

This book is to be returned on or before
the last date stamped below.

LIBREX